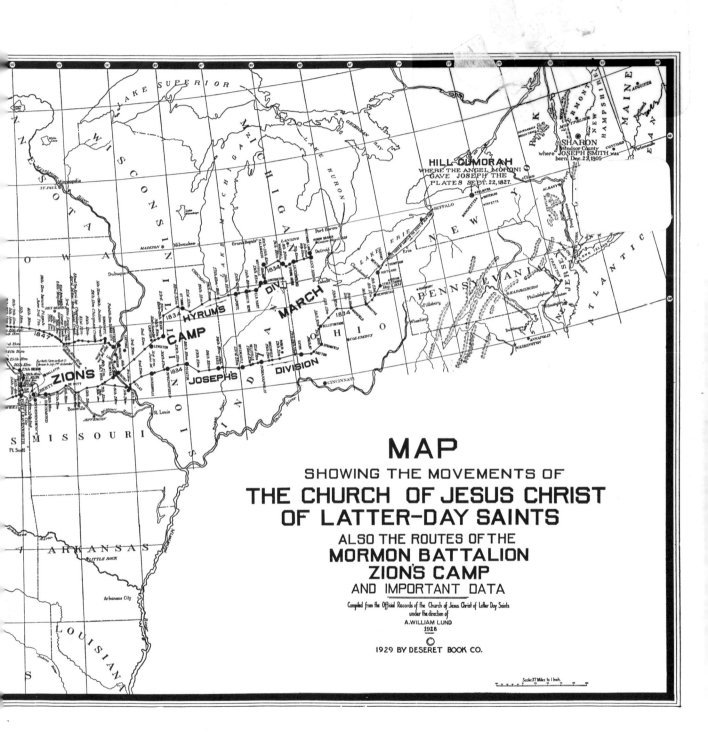

MAP

SHOWING THE MOVEMENTS OF

THE CHURCH OF JESUS CHRIST
OF LATTER-DAY SAINTS

ALSO THE ROUTES OF THE

MORMON BATTALION
ZION'S CAMP

AND IMPORTANT DATA

Compiled from the Official Records of the Church of Jesus Christ of Latter Day Saints
under the direction of
A. WILLIAM LUND
1928

Ⓒ

1929 BY DESERET BOOK CO.

Scale: 37 Miles to 1 Inch.

The

HISTORY
of the
MORMONS

The
HISTORY
of the
MORMONS

IN PHOTOGRAPHS AND TEXT: 1830 TO THE PRESENT

Douglas F. Tobler
Nelson B. Wadsworth

ST. MARTIN'S PRESS   NEW YORK

German language edition published by Swan Buch-Vertrieb GmbH in 1987 under the title *Der Weg zum Licht.*

BOOK DESIGN BY JUDITH STAGNITTO.

Library of Congress Cataloging-in-Publication Data

Tobler, Douglas F.
    The history of the Mormons : in photographs and text : 1830 to the
present / Douglas F. Tobler and Nelson B. Wadsworth.
      p.   cm.
   ISBN 0-312-03359-1
   1. Mormon Church—History.   2. Church of Jesus Christ of Latter-
Day Saints—History.   3. Mormon Church—History—Pictorial works.
4. Church of Jesus Christ of Latter Day Saints—History—Pictorial
works.   I. Wadsworth, Nelson B., 1930–   .   II. Title.
BX8611.T63 1989
289.3'09—dc20   89-32762
                                                CIP

First Edition

10 9 8 7 6 5 4 3 2 1

Contents

$\mathcal{I}$NTRODUCTION

"And in the days of these kings shall the God of heaven set up a kingdom, which shall never be destroyed: and the kingdom shall not be left to other people, but it shall break in pieces and consume all these kingdoms, and it shall stand forever."
—Daniel 2:44

"In the 150 years since these obscure beginnings, the Mormons have sustained the most rapid growth of any new religious movement in American history. Indeed, today they stand on the threshold of becoming the first major new world *faith to appear since the Prophet Mohammed rode out of the desert."*
—Rodney Stark
The Rise of a New World Faith

"Mormonism holds up a different goal: (eternal progression) toward godhood. When this theological conception is added to the peculiar understanding that Saints have of themselves and their Hebraic-Christianness, which grew out of their past as peculiar people, it becomes clear as can be that nomenclature notwithstanding, Mormonism is a new religious tradition."
—Jan Shipps
Mormonism: The Story of a New Religious Tradition

A few years ago a German publisher, Cajo Liesenberg, contacted us about doing a photographic history of the Mormons in German. He and a friend, Arne Bohle, had already begun a collection of some representative photographs drawn from several archival sources, including the archives of the Church of Jesus Christ of Latter-day Saints, the Utah State Historical Society, and Brigham Young University. Then, Nelson provided the bulk of the photographs from his own substantial Mormon archive, collected over twenty years of research in frontier photography. As committed Latter-day Saints eager to share our heritage with a worldwide audience, we were enthusiastic about the project from the beginning. We wish to express our sincere appreciation to Cajo for giving us this opportunity and are now pleased that this work will appear in English.

Many friends have helped us along the way; we owe them a debt of gratitude. William Slaughter of the Church Archives; Dennis Rowley, Brigham Young University archivist; and A.J. Simmonds of Utah State University gave aid and encouragement in locating some photographs. Bradley Olsen and Jeffrey Anderson helped with some of the research. Maureen Beecher and Thomas Alexander read and improved the text. We thank all of them for their suggestions and friendship. They are not responsible for the book and whatever shortcomings it may have.

We also thank all of our editors at St. Martin's Press, especially Barbara Anderson and Anne Savarese, for the pleasure of working with them and for the improvements they have brought to this English edition.

FREEZING MOMENTS OF TIME

Men with cameras have been documenting their times since the first practical form of photography was introduced to mankind by Louis Jacques Mandé Daguerre in Paris, France, in 1839. The daguerreotype, as this revolutionary discovery of science was known, and its successor, the collodion wet plate process, quickly spread around the globe, even to some of the most remote outposts of civilization. Despite the cumbersome nature of their technology, talented photographers have always been among the pioneers . . . the first to set up shop in the frontier communities . . . the first to explore America's western wilderness . . . the first to climb her mountain peaks . . . the first to navigate her wild rivers . . . the first to bring the visual realities of people, places and events to the doorsteps of the world.[1]

Prior to 1839, visual documentation was confined to the creativity of artists, with their often vivid imaginations and their widely varied skills at converting observations and thoughts into drawings, sketches, paintings, and other visual representations. The resulting artwork was often colored and sensationalized by the prejudices and biases of the artists who worked somewhere in the nebulous realm between fact, fantasy, and fiction.

But photography changed all of that. With its invention there was a more truthful medium of visual reportage available to mankind, one that was based more on objectivity and the real world than on the artist's fancy, one that could convey reality rather than sensational stereotype.[2]

Louis Jacques Mandé Daguerre, the so-called "father of photography," poses in Charles R. Meade's daguerreotype studio in New York City in 1848. This photographic copy of the original daguerreotype was found in the scrapbook of Utah photographer Charles R. Savage.

Following the discoveries of Daguerre and fellow Frenchman Joseph Nicéphore Niépce and English contemporary William Henry Fox Talbot, it suddenly became possible to capture images from life in a magic little black box. The optical ability of glass lenses, mounted on the so-called camera obscura, to refract points of light and create images had long been known to man, but prior to 1839 it had not been possible to retain them. The pioneer inventors of photography took the camera obscura, coupled it with the peculiar chemical characteristics of silver, and made it possible not only to "freeze" moments of time but also, through the magic of chemistry, to make those moments permanent.

From that day forward humankind became a "seeing" creature, and photography quickly evolved into a useful tool in its hands, not only to titillate the visual senses but to document the truth and reality of its history and to transmit them into the future so generations not yet born could see what it was like to live in its times.

As photography was taking root in America and creating its visual consciousness among the people, a peculiar religion was also establishing itself on the frontier, a religion that would in the years to come grow and expand around the world and in the process lend itself well to the newfound elements of photo documentation. The Church of Jesus Christ of Latter-day Saints, or "the Mormons" as the sect was known, had its humble beginnings in upstate New York in 1830. By the time photography was introduced in New York City ten years later, the Mormons had grown substantially in numbers and were struggling on the western frontier to build a progressive, utopian city on the banks of the Mississippi River at Nauvoo, Illinois. New converts from Europe were already streaming into "Nauvoo, City Beautiful," to establish their homes, to practice their new-found faith, and to create a massive melting pot of religious humanity in America.

Even though the Mormon Church was a true American religion and was putting down solid roots in the rich, western Illinois soil, early in its history, at the urging of its Prophet, it had sent missionaries around the globe to, as the Prophet had proclaimed, "preach the Gospel to every nation, kindred, tongue and people on the face of the earth."[3] It was perhaps this zeal to share their religion with the rest of the world, coupled with some "peculiar" Mormon practices like polygamy, divine revelation, the tithe, and literal adherance to other Old and New Testament doctrines, that led to their persecution, mob violence, the murder of their prophet and eventual expulsion of the Latter-day Saints from Missouri and Illinois. The persecutions also encouraged the growing sect to continue migrating west to a desolate land in the Great Basin and Rocky Mountains, a land no one else wanted at the time, but a land where Mormons believed they could practice their religion in peace.

The utopian Mormon city of Nauvoo, Illinois, rises from the banks of the Mississippi River. This old engraving, drawn around 1844–1845, looks from Montrose, Iowa, toward "the City Beautiful" with its Mormon Temple under construction at the crest of the hill.

This early daguerreotype camera, copied from an old 1840s manual, is similar to the ones used by the first daguerreotypists in Nauvoo and Utah.

Below: A "daguerreotype outfit" is pictured in this old woodcut from a daguerreotype manual printed in 1847 by J. Thierry. Making daguerreotypes was a complex, expensive venture that required use of specialized apparatus.

There were cameramen among the Latter-day Saints documenting their travails, their great westward migration, and their building up of what they unabashedly to this day call "the Kingdom of God" or the "latter-day Zion" in the tops of the mountains of Utah. The daguerreotypist, of course, was the first to photographically record the Mormon scene.

While daguerreotypists were indeed at work in Nauvoo as early as the spring of 1844, few images of that early Mormon period survive, mainly because the daguerreotype, being a one-time, unreproducible image, was quickly carried away by the client and was too easily lost among the material belongings of family. They had no more chance of survival than a locket or piece of jewelry. Those that did manage to survive are found mostly in the archives of the Mormon Church in Salt Lake City or in private collections.

Because daguerreotypes are mirror-like, are subject to silver tarnishing, and appear like negative images when held at certain angles to the reflected light, they are often not appreciated by those who look upon them.[4] It is only through careful, enhanced copy work that the clarity of the true moment frozen by the photographer can be fully realized, published, and enjoyed by the masses.[5]

Suffice it to say that the original daguerreotypes had incredible resolution, were virtually grainless and were probably the most beautiful form of photography ever invented. But a daguerreotype plagued by age and tarnish and endlessly rattled about in a family's hand-me-downs can become practically invisible, and although the original image is still there just waiting to emerge, it doesn't appear to the naked eye to be anything of much value. For this reason, the vast majority of the daguerreotypes taken in frontier communities like

Timothy O'Sullivan, a government photographer on several geographical surveys in Utah and the West, stands in front of his collodion wet-plate darkroom tent in this old woodcut engraved from a photograph taken on the King Survey. Although the original photograph has been lost, the woodcut print probably accurately portrays the scene.

Nauvoo have been lost forever. Nevertheless, there are still many remarkable images out there in various hiding places awaiting discovery, including, possibly, a daguerreotype portrait of the Mormon Prophet-founder Joseph Smith, which for more than three-quarters of a century has eluded researchers and historians.[6]

Daguerreotype images are indeed fragile and can easily be rubbed or erased from their mirror-like, polished surfaces. They are nevertheless made of durable, long-lasting materials—silver, polished to a high lustre, on a copper plate, sensitized in the vapors of iodine and developed in the fumes of mercury. Unfortunately, many valuable images have been destroyed by unknowing people who attempted to clean or polish off the silver tarnish. Daguerreotypes can be cleaned, but modern conservators disagree on whether or not they should be subjected to any such chemical processes.[7] At any rate, cleaning involves great risk to the daguerreotype image and novices should not attempt it. If the decision is made to clean, it should be done by a technical expert who knows what he or she is doing, and a good copy of the image should be made before the process is started because there is a risk of losing it entirely.[8]

With proper care, kept in their velvet-lined leather cases and beneath a brass frame and sheet of protecting glass, daguerreotypes can survive for centuries and in the process convey a great deal of visual information to future generations about nineteenth century America and her people.

The survivability of photographic images was greatly enhanced in the 1850s with the discovery that collodion or "gun cotton," a gummy fluid previously used in medicine to cover wounds, could be used as a vehicle or emulsion to hold light-sensitive materials on a glass plate. This led to the development of ambrotypes, the so-called "daguerreotypes on glass," and finally to wet-plate photography, an era that lasted for more than a quarter of a century. Collodion photography produced a negative on glass that could be used to reproduce multiple images on light-sensitive paper

The accurate image of an unidentified pioneer Mormon couple bridges the gap of time. Despite numerous scratches and abrasions on the polished silver daguerreotype plate, the image has survived more than 135 years.

emulsions. Albumen, a durable, viscous fluid derived from egg whites, was commonly sensitized in a silver nitrate solution to produce long-lasting paper prints capable of surviving under archival storage conditions for more than a century. The archival nature of the materials and the careful techniques of many photographers virtually ensured the survival of many decisive moments of history.[9]

It has always been a source of amazement that many wet-plate photographers among the Mormons, from Marsena Cannon to William Henry Jackson, from Charles Roscoe Savage to Jack Hillers and Timothy O'Sullivan, carried their heavy cameras and darkroom equipment into the field in wagons and on pack mules to photo-document the western frontier during its most intense and difficult period of history, when much of it was undiscovered wilderness inhabited by hostile Indians.

Wet-plate photography was extremely complex and difficult because the photographer had to take everything with him to the landscapes and people he wanted to photograph. The technology required preparing and sensitizing the plates, exposing them, and developing the negatives within a span of twenty minutes, while they were still wet and tacky. Otherwise, they were rendered insensitive and the photograph ended in failure. Yet, despite a plethora of technical problems inherent in the process, those who did practice the art and its necessary science did a remarkably thorough job of photo-documenting the exploration of the West and Mormon settlement of the frontier.[10]

Finding visual images of the growth and expansion of the Mormon Church around the world has indeed been a fascinating pastime. In the twenty years we have been collecting, first for the Utah Historical Society, then for the Harold B. Lee Library at Brigham Young University, and now for the library at Utah State University, we have been constantly amazed at the depth and completeness of the photographic documentation. Photographs were indeed taken of nearly every major event in Mormondom since 1844, with the exception, perhaps, of the initial trek to the Great Salt Lake Valley in 1847.[11]

Literally hundreds of thousands of images lie somewhere—in public and private collections, in family photo albums, in old attics, under the dust of ages in ramshackle sheds and garages, even beneath a tattered canvas in an abandoned chicken coop, where we once found more than 6,000 glass negatives waiting to be discovered and brought out into the light of day.

We have also been intrigued by the immensity of the task of pulling together historic photographs. The more we find the more we realize are yet to be found. It recently dawned on us that we could spend our whole lifetimes collecting photographica and never do more than merely scratch the surface. The biggest frustration seems to center around the ease with which excellent photographs are discarded and lost forever to history. Frequently the trail of a photographer's work terminates in a dead end with this matter-of-fact comment from an indifferent relative: "Oh, those old glass plates were carted off to the dump a long time ago." Such an attitude has always puzzled us, particularly after finding choice photographic images on old glass negatives in someone's trash. When one prints these clear, detailed, high-resolution photographs from the photographer's original negatives, the people and landscapes in them immediately come to life, putting flesh on the skeletons of history and breathing life into the ghosts of people who once walked the earth like we do.

Despite the frustrations of lost photographs, I [Nelson B. Wadsworth] have been able to amass in 20 years, conservatively speaking, close to 200,000 photographs of Utah and Mormon scenes, including many original negatives, which I deem to be the choicest photographic legacy because like-original prints can be made from them. Most of these images are now carefully preserved and are held in safe keeping in various Utah archives. Unfortunately, because of a lack of funds, the majority of them, particularly the negatives, are yet uncatalogued and are merely in an unused state of preservation. My philosophy has been to get them preserved and protected before someone decides to throw them away.

Jack Hillers works with his collodion wet-plate equipment on the Aquarius Plateau in Utah during the Powell Survey of the Colorado Plateau in 1872. The photograph was taken by James Fennemore, a Mormon photographer who taught Hillers photography.

The first portrait of Brigham Young in Utah was taken December 14, 1850, in the Old Fort in Salt Lake City by Marsena Cannon, Utah's first photographer. This particular photograph was copied from the original daguerreotype in the Mormon Church's historical collection.

A photo copy of another Cannon daguerreotype of Brigham Young, left, can be compared to Frederick Hawkins Piercy's steel engraving made from the same daguerreotype, right. The engraving was published in 1853, dating the image sometime between 1850 and 1853.

From that massive collection, for this book, I printed nearly 4,000 images in the darkroom. These were edited down to 1,000 working photographs, from which the final selections were eventually made, selections that, I hope, visually tell the story of the dramatic rise of the Mormon Church from a small sect to a powerful, influential, worldwide religion with more than 6 million members—and still growing by leaps and bounds.

During the editing process, I was continually impressed with the ability of a single black-and-white photograph to somehow survive the ages. Many, of course, did not endure, particularly the original negatives. It was common for a photographer's negatives to quickly vanish after his death, but his photographs can still survive through prints handed down from generation to generation. Naturally, with the original negatives gone, there is a continual erosion of quality because the images can continue to survive only through facsimile photo copying. With each new generation of copying, the resolution fades and the image loses its touch with reality.

Despite the perceived, so-called permanence of photographic images, they were and still are, at best, somewhat fragile, tenuous things. Like all material objects, photographs created today are destined eventually to return to the dust from whence they came. Those that do survive for future generations are still at the mercy of the elements to which they are subjected, including a variety of abuses at the touch of human hands. No matter what preservation techniques are used, the aging-fading process continues its inexorable toll, the speed and degree of this erosion of time depending on the archival nature of the storage.

And to compound the survival problem, the technology of photography has gone backward instead of forward in the archival permanence of the materials used in making modern photographs. Photographers of yesteryear were much more conscious of archival processing and preservation than those of today. Scientific development of "living color," as sensational as it was to the visual senses, was a giant leap backward in permanence, mainly because of rapid fading characteristics of the dyes used in modern color emulsions.

Albumen, silver nitrate, and gold chloride, key ingredients in pioneer photography, were ideally suited for archival permanence. On the other hand, dyes used in the layered couplers of most modern color emulsions quickly fade, and in a matter of just a few decades, the frozen moments become dim and indistinguishable, and the paper and film carriers of the color emulsions are all that are left behind.[12]

The non-archival nature of color was quickly made apparent to me early in my photo collecting. Back in the late 1960s, when I was working on a master's thesis on frontier photography at the University of Utah, the late historian Charles Kelly, who was a credible photographer, gave me a large box of early color transparencies he had taken in the 1930s and 1940s of a variety of Utah scenes. When I got home I eagerly opened the box to see what Charlie had given me. What a disappointment! Most of the color had faded to a faint, barely discernible, unreproducible, magenta image. Charlie's collection of slides had been rendered useless by poor photographic technology and the erosion of time. Today it's even worse. Photo manufacturers prefer to cut corners on the ingredients in their materials than to produce products aimed at an archival permanence. Even the black and white materials are beginning to be non-archival, as manufacturers cut down on the silver content of their emulsions and convince photographers to use resin-coated papers rather than those with a longer-lasting fiber base.

Unfortunately, that is much of the legacy modern photographers will leave future generations: faded color and black-and-white images to document our times. The other day, while editing a folder full of the earliest-known photographs in the Mormon Church, actually facsimile copies of early daguerreotypes, I suddenly realized if the photographers of 138 years ago had been using our modern color emulsions, nothing of their work would remain, and a great gap would exist in the photo-documentation of the Mormon Church. As I stood at the editing table, I picked up a clear portrait of Brigham Young, the first known photograph taken in Salt Lake City. I looked into the face of that great colonizer, whose contributions as a spiritual leader and economic organizer are unequaled in western history. Suddenly it became quite clear to me that the photographer who took the picture, and those who followed in his footsteps, have bridged the gap in time and helped me come face-to-face with Brigham Young. This particular photograph tells us precisely what he looked like on December 12, 1850, as he sat before Marsena Cannon's camera in the Old Fort in the fledgling frontier settlement of Great Salt Lake City, Territory of Utah.

Those photographers, many of them now unknown, have left an incredible visual record for us and future generations of what it was like to live in their times.

I picked up another full-body view of Parley P. Pratt (see page 13). It was probably taken in the same year and possibly on the same day as Brigham Young's portrait. It instantly jerked me back to Cannon's crude studio in the Old Fort. There is a mysterious air of reality in that image as a tight-lipped Apostle Pratt faces the camera, his large left hand clutching a draped chair. You can even see Cannon's crude, neutral-colored backdrop behind the subject and the legs of the neck clamp that immobilized him during the long exposure. I almost expected Pratt to suddenly breathe a sigh and say, "Come on, old chap, have you had enough?"

At the time Cannon was taking these pictures in Utah, in Washington, D.C., another daguerreotypist named Mathew Brady was preparing to publish his *Gallery of Illustrious Americans*. These were actually to be daguerreotype portraits of "the 24 most eminent citizens of the American republic since the death of President Washington," copied on lithographic stone by the well-known contemporary artist Francis D'Avignon. Only twelve of Brady's *Illustrious Americans* were actually ever published, but in Utah, Marsena Cannon and other daguerreotypists were producing at the same time what I like to call *A Gallery of Illustrious Pioneers*. Many of those portraits, too, were engraved and lithographed from Marsena Cannon's daguerreotypes by the English artist Frederick Hawkins Piercy, first as a finely printed display piece called the "Plate of the First Presidency and the Twelve Apostles of The Church of Jesus Christ of Latter-day Saints" in 1853 and two years later in his classic book for Mormon emigrants, *Route from Liverpool to Great Salt Lake Valley*.[13] We begin this photographic work with a selection of those choice daguerreotypes, as well as some others, many of which are published here for the first time. And with them, hopefully, we can take the reader back in time.

Mormon Apostle Parley P. Pratt faces Marsena Cannon's daguerreotype camera in the Old Fort in Great Salt Lake City sometime in 1850.

erleaf, pages 14–15: A photographer and his helper make collodion wet-plate photographs in the field in this engraving from *A History* *Handbook of Photography*, published in 1877. Although the technology required the photographer to take his darkroom with him wherever went, many used the process to photo-document the exploration of the wilderness and the settlement of the West.

Three small pioneer children in Great Salt Lake City have their portrait taken by daguerreotype sometime in the early 1850s.

DAGUERREOTYPING.

I AM now ready to execute Daguerreotype Likenesses in the most approved style of the Art, with all the late improvements, in the building at the north east corner of the "Old Fort," sixth ward, fitted up expressly for the purpose, with a large sky light, so that the work can be done equally as well in foul weather as fair. Particular pains taken with Likenesses of children. Having had nine years practice in the Art, principally in the city of Boston, Mass., I fancy I can suit the most discriminating taste. All persons are invited to call and see specimens of work.

   References,—W. Woodruff, of the Twelve, W. W. Phelps, Heywood & Woolley, E. Whipple, and A. Badlam.

                M. CANNON.

Dec. 10, 1850.-22tf

The first daguerreotyping services among the Mormons on the western frontier were offered in these advertisements, left, in the *Deseret News* in 1850 by Marsena Cannon, a veteran daguerreotypist from Boston, and by William A. Smith, right, in the *Frontier Guardian* in Kanesville, Iowa, in 1852. Smith announces he has in his possession "daguerrean pictures" of Joseph and Hyrum Smith, which were more than likely daguerreotype copies of oil paintings.

posite left and above: The difference of three years of living on
frontier can be seen in a comparison of these two daguerreotype
traits of Wilford Woodruff. The one above was taken in 1850
Marsena Cannon in Plumbe's Daguerreotype Gallery in Boston.
e one on page 18 was taken by Cannon in Salt Lake City in 1853.

ght and top right: Two other portraits of Woodruff family mem-
s taken in 1850 in Boston by Marsena Cannon show Wilford's
e, Phoebe, and his son, Wilford, Jr., age 10.

Above: Another Wilford Woodruff family portrait, was proba[bly] taken in 1848 or 1849 in Boston by Marsena Cannon. In his jour[nal] Woodruff recorded on March 14, 1849, "I also received a pres[ent] from Br. Cannon of two Degoritype [sic] likenesses of mys[elf,] wife, and three children in a family groupe." Although Woodr[uff] appears older in this portrait, his son, Wilford, Jr., looks to be ab[out] 8 or 9.

Opposite right: An unidentified mother has her daguerreotype tak[en] with her two daughters who are clothed in similar dresses. T[his] photo, copied from the original in the LDS Church collection, [was] taken by one of several daguerreotypists operating in Salt Lake C[ity] in the 1850s.

Left: An unidentified Mormon girl is pictured in this daguerreoty[pe] circa 1855.

THE FIRST PRESIDENCY
AND
THE TWELVE APOSTLES.
A.D. 1853.

Mormon Apostle Erastus Snow stands stiffly in Marsena Cannon's gallery in 1850, shortly after he served on a committee to draft the Constitution for the State of Deseret. (LDS Church Historical Department daguerreotype collection)

Apostle Orson Hyde stands stiffly for his daguerreotype portrait precisely the same studio setting as Apostles Pratt and Kimball (s pages 13 and 22), circa 1850.

Page 22: Heber C. Kimball, a member of the Mormon Church's First Presidency, poses in a broad coat in Marsena Cannon's studio in the Old Fort, circa 1850. Note the books placed under the head clamp stand just behind Kimball's feet.

Page 23: Leaders of the Mormon Church are pictured in a series of steel engravings made from Marsena Cannon daguerreotypes by English artist Frederick Hawkins Piercy and published in Liverpool, England, in 1853 by Samuel W. Richards, then president of the British Mission and editor of the Mormon periodical *The Millennial Star*.

Opposite right: Apostle Ezra Taft Benson, great grandfather of pr ent-day Mormon Church President Ezra Taft Benson, is pictured this official portrait taken in 1853 by Marsena Cannon in Salt La City. The photo was copied from the original daguerreotype.

...asa M. Lyman is pictured around 1850 in this daguerreotype by ...rsena Cannon. Lyman, a leader in the western exodus, served in ... Quorum of the 12 Apostles for many years but was excommun- ...ed in 1870 "for preaching false doctrine." (LDS Historical De- ...tment daguerreotype collection)

Polly Walworth Lambson wears typical pioneer attire in this early 1850s daguerreotype portrait.

...posite left: Apostle Lorenzo Snow is photographed in Marsena ...nnon's gallery about 1850, when he is in his mid-30s. During his ... he served missions for his church in Italy, Switzerland, Malta, ...ia, and Hawaii. He would also later become President of the ...S Church, serving from 1898 until his death in 1901. (LDS His- ...ical Department daguerreotype collection)

Elisa Rebecca Robinson Wells, first wife of Mormon leader Daniel H. Wells, is shown in this ⅛th-plate daguerreotype, circa 1853.

Lillian Lyon Staines, wife of William C. Staines, poses quaintly for Marsena Cannon in 1854. This photo is copied from the original, hand-colored daguerreotype in the LDS Church collection.

lard Young, son of Brigham Young, is pictured in full uniform ge 17. He attended West Point Academy, became a commised officer in the U.S. Army, and eventually fought in the Spanish-erican War.

Utah poetess Eliza R. Snow, one of the plural wives of Brigham Young, is photographed by Marsena Cannon sometime in the mid-1850s.

posite left: Mary Ann Angel Young, one of the 19 wives of gham Young, is portrayed in typical pioneer dress of the 1850s his photo copied from the original daguerreotype.

John Smith, patriarch to the Mormon Church, clutches a cane in this daguerreotype taken by Marsena Cannon shortly before the patriarch's death. Smith was the Prophet Joseph Smith's uncle.

Joseph F. Smith, who would later become President of the Morm Church, is pictured at age 19 shortly after he returned home fr a mission to the Hawaiian Islands in 1857.

Opposite right: Pioneer Mormon Bishop H. Kesler poses in a guerreotype gallery in his Nauvoo Legion uniform. Kesler acquir a page from the original manuscript of the Book of Mormon (page 62), which has been preserved in the University of Utah chives. The page was recently found in Kesler's possessions hand down through members of his family. Copied from the origi daguerreotype. (University of Utah Western Americana Collecti Salt Lake City)

Above: An unidentified pioneer family peer across the ages in this portrait taken sometime in the 1860s. The original was copied from a tintype, the collodion process in which the image was made on black japanned tin instead of glass.

Opposite left: Joseph Smith III, son of the Mormon prophet, is shown in a daguerreotype portrait taken sometime around 1860, when he accepted the presidency of the Reorganized Church of Jesus Christ of Latter-day Saints, whose organizers believed in the "lineal descent" of the Church presidency from father to son.

Right: Orrin Porter Rockwell, the so-called Mormon Destroying Angel, sported locks of long, shoulder-length hair, a trademark he would carry through his life.

An Obsession Fulfilled

*I*n the twenty years that I [Nelson B. Wadsworth] have been collecting images, many people involved in different aspects of historical documentation have been helpful to me in this work. People like Dennis Rowley, the talented archivist at BYU, Mrs. Elizabeth Winters, John F. Bennett's daughter, and Mrs. Ivor Clark Sharp, one of Photographer C.R. Savage's granddaughters, were particularly helpful in the initial research. They helped to mold the vision in me for documentary photography. But probably the most important contributor, at least in my view, has long been dead, and I never met him, although I feel I know him intimately. At least I believe I got somewhat close to his personality through many years of uncovering his photographs, examining them closely, becoming aware of his unique style and, finally, printing his negatives. He died two years before I was born, yet the photography he left behind and the example he set have taught me a great deal about visual documentation. I shall ever be grateful to him for the obsession he expressed in his diaries and displayed in his work in documenting the Mormon scene.

I'm talking about George Edward Anderson, the talented Springville, Utah, photographer, who seemed to anticipate this book long before our time. In fact, there is even something mysterious and uncanny about his photographs and the way he went with his camera to the very roots of Mormonism. For me at least, the pieces of the puzzle he provided some eight decades ago are now falling into place. Of course, many of the images he created have already been published in various books and periodicals, particularly in recent years because there has been a rediscovery of his art. But nobody to my knowledge has attempted to publish what Anderson really intended and was obsessed with shortly after the turn of the century. He wanted to thoroughly document *The Birth of Mormonism*,

to publish a comprehensive visual history of The Church of Jesus Christ of Latter-day Saints, precisely what we are attempting to do in this book.

We couldn't ask for any better photographs if we had sent our own, modern-day photographer on assignment to do the same thing. But Anderson went on assignment for no one, yet there seemed to be direction and vision in his work. He seemed to know exactly what he wanted to say in his pictures and was, in a sense, a photojournalist ahead of his time.

Anderson traveled "without purse or script" on his four-year *Birth of Mormonism* hiatus from his normal Utah gallery work, earning his way as he went along with his camera, tarrying with commercial portraiture for long periods near the historic Mormon sites, so he could earn enough money to continue on his Quixotic obsession to document the roots of his church.

It all began when the talented photographer, at age forty-six, was called on a mission to England for the Mormon Church in the spring of 1907. He saw the call as an answer to a prayer, a prayer that he might be able to use his camera to serve God and Zion. He asked for, and received, permission from the Church to make detours on his way east to photograph some of the historic sites central to the roots of Mormonism. A clue to his obsession to do so is contained in his diary now in the archives at Brigham Young University: "I feel so impressed with the necessity of making the views," he wrote. "I can see what a blessing they would be to our people in arousing an interest in this land, and the work that is before us as a people in building up the centre stake of Zion."

To him, his work was like a spiritual calling, and he pursued it with a vigor and enthusiasm that explains the prolific photographic heritage he ultimately created and left behind. His concentration was so intense and his vision so far ahead of his time that few, if any, understood what he was about. Ultimately it resulted in neglect of his family for at least four years and bruised his marital relation-

Opposite left, and page 38: Photographer George Edward Anderson, left, as a young man about age 20, wears his Sunday school attire and, page 38, clads himself in clothes for working in the field. He preferred field, documentary photography to studio work, and produced most of the "Birth of Mormonism" photos. (Photos by either Stanley or Adam Anderson, George Edward's brothers, who also pursued careers in photography.)

ship to a degree from which it never fully recovered, although his religious upbringing would never allow a divorce. And what did he get for all of this sacrifice and anguish? Practically nothing. In all of his hard work, he never ever really made money with his talent and was so poor in his financial dealings that he died practically penniless. Yet, the art of his photography, at least the human interest of it, is probably unequalled.

"Dad didn't go right out and take pictures like most photographers," said his daughter, Eva Noyes, in 1974. "He would visit the spot he wanted to photograph and walk through it and around it for hours, deciding the exact time for the best lighting to make his negatives."[14]

And so it was with his photo-documentation of the historic Church sites. He was slow and meticulous, and it took so long that eventually the delay in going to England became an embarrassment to his family. Anderson was still in New York in June of 1908, ten months after he had departed Springville. A month later he finally boarded a steamer and went to England, but three years later, his mission concluded, he didn't bother to go home.

He simply returned to New England and picked up where he had left off on his obsession.

In all, Anderson was absent from his Springville gallery for more than seven years, only three of which were spent in England on his mission.[15]

The Deseret Sunday School Union, an auxiliary of the Mormon Church, published a book of Anderson's photographs of historic sites in 1909, even before the photographer returned to Utah. But *The Birth of Mormonism in Picture, Scenes and Incidents in Early Church History*, was more of a pamphlet than a book, although it does contain some finely reproduced, duotone-like engravings of some of his best photographs. It was, however, more of a proselyting tool than an attempt at visual documentation.[16]

And so it is that we borrow heavily from Anderson's work. As we envision it, this work is merely an extension of the photographer's dream. We think he would have liked it, not only because we lean heavily on his art, but because it is our attempt to carry on his efforts of eighty years ago. And so, let us take you back.

Below: Photographer George Edward Anderson, left, and a missionary companion push their suitcases on a cart during a move from one city to another in England in 1909. A year later Anderson returned to New England to continue his photo documentation of the roots of Mormonism. (Photo postcard Anderson sent home to his family, courtesy Eva Noyes)

The Roots of Mormonism

On April 6, 1830 six young men—Joseph, Hyrum, and Samuel Smith; Peter and David Whitmer; and Oliver Cowdery—met with others in a small frontier farmhouse in rural western New York to officially found what later became known as the Church of Jesus Christ of Latter-day Saints (Mormons). It was an inauspicious beginning for a church that during most of its existence in the nineteenth and twentieth centuries would be considered a "sect," hardly to be taken seriously by the rest of the Christian, let alone the non-Christian world.

But much has changed, especially within recent decades. Scholars and laymen alike are pausing to inquire who Mormons are and what Mormonism teaches. Looking at Mormon growth patterns over the past century and a half, non-Mormon sociologist Rodney Stark has called Mormonism "a new religion, a new world faith," one that ". . . will soon achieve a worldwide following comparable to that of Islam, Buddhism, Christianity, Hinduism, and the other dominant world faiths." For scholars as well as curious students of religion throughout the world, Stark continued, the Mormon "miracle" represents ". . . one of the great events in the history of religion." (Stark, 18, 27)

For non-Mormon historian Jan Shipps, Mormonism is a "new religious tradition" that "differs from traditional Christianity in much the same fashion that traditional Christianity, in its ultimate emphasis on the individual, came to differ from Judaism." (Shipps, 148) She, too, calls for broader study and deeper understanding of the Mormon phenomenon.

A granite monument and Memorial Cottage mark the spot in Sharon, Windsor County, Vermont, where Joseph Smith, Jr., was born. The monument was dedicated December 23, 1905, the 100th anniversary of the Mormon prophet's birth. (Photo by George Edward Anderson, 1907)

It was the church's unusual statistics that first arrested Stark's attention. From the original six, Mormon membership had, by 1988, grown to well over 6 million worldwide. By 1980, he noted, Mormons had become the fifth largest body in the United States, surpassing Episcopalians, Presbyterians ". . . and even the Lutherans." Only the Roman Catholic Church, two Baptist churches, and the United Methodist Church were larger. More important to this sociologist of religion, however, was the dynamism manifest not so much in the numbers as in the rate of growth: for the 1970s it was 73 percent, for the early 1980s, 58 percent. Stark concluded from these figures that if the

Mormon Church should continue to grow by an average of 30 percent per decade, there would be 60 million Mormons throughout the world in 2080. A 50 percent rate would push Mormon membership to 265 million, a dizzying possibility, to say the least.

This growth did not come easily, but rather in the face of persistent persecution in virtually every country where Mormons entered to proselyte and, more recently, against the more powerful forces of secularization. "Mormons thrive in the most, not the least, secularized nations," Stark wrote. Contrary to some widely held views, he continued ". . . Mormons [do not] mainly find their converts among the poor and dispossessed, those least affected by modernization and the onset of secularization" but "as with new religious movements generally appeal most effectively to the better educated and more successful." (Stark, 22–27)

This book is a photographic history of the transformation of the church from a "sect" to a "world faith" and the people who brought it about. From humble beginnings as just one of many religious movements that sprang up mushroom-like from the fertile soil of nineteenth century America, Mormons have gradually extended themselves into much of the world.

This is their story in photo and text, the story of a church, a people, a worldwide community bound together in love and spirit by a common faith, common commitments, and, above all, a common doctrine of God and man, heaven, and earth.

This common faith and doctrine is the primary and powerful thread of continuity amid change that ties the first Mormon, Joseph Smith, to the latest convert in Korea, Nigeria, or Germany. Here are the faces, the places, the monuments, the visual images that mirror that powerful continuity and also the development of this people with their struggles, persecutions, and achievements. This is the visual story of an every-growing group of overwhelmingly common people who, through faith and toil, built up the church—to them God's kingdom—under difficult circumstances first in America and then into other parts of the world. Much of it is told through the lenses of talented photographers—some Mormon, some not—who

captured on film both what they saw and what they felt. Some of the story will be recounted by those who helped make the history, and in their own words; some by interested onlookers fascinated by a "different," even peculiar people.

Opposite right: Lucy Mack Smith, mother of the Mormon Prophet Joseph Smith, is sketched from life by Frederick Hawkins Piercy. The artist used a "camera lucida" to make the portrait. (Taken from Route from Liverpool to Great Salt Lake Valley)

Below: Paintings of Lucy Mack Smith and her sons, Hyrum and Joseph, are hung above the mantel in the Memorial Cottage near South Royalton, Vermont, where the Mormon Prophet Joseph Smith was born in 1805. (Photo by George Edward Anderson)

NO. 51.

The contrasts of fall and winter are reflected in these two pictures of Tunbridge, Vermont, taken in 1907–1908 by Springville, Utah, photographer George Edward Anderson. Joseph Smith, Sr., and Lucy Mack cultivated a farm here after their marriage in 1796, establishing the roots of Mormonism and the start of a new church.

Cows graze beneath the "O[ld]
Elm" at Dairy Hill Far[m],
South Royalton, Vermont, [as]
George Edward Anderson [cap]-
tures his landscape in his [cam]-
era in 1908. The elm stoo[d at]
the Smith Farm when Jo[seph]
was a boy.

An old couple pose with t[heir]
oxen in front of the Har[vey]
Smith home in Vermont. Sm[ith]
was an early convert to [the]
Mormon Church and a rela[tive]
of the prophet. (Photo [by]
George Edward Anderson[.])

46

Left: Two elderly New Englanders pause on a country lane in front of uncle Ben C. Latham's home in Vermont, where Joseph Smith grew up and spent his childhood years. (Photo by George Edward Anderson)

Overleaf, pages 48–49: Tombstones mark the graves of the Smith family near Tunbridge, Vermont. Ancestors of Joseph and Hyrum Smith are buried in this cemetery. (Photo by George Edward Anderson, 1907)

Below: An old wood-frame, one-room schoolhouse stands in Vermont in 1908 when Springville photographer George Edward Anderson visually records historic Mormon sites. Joseph Smith is said to have attended school in this building when he was a boy growing up in New England.

3A

THE FOUNDING IN NEW YORK

An understanding of the foundations of Mormonism is a key to understanding the people, their motivation, and their achievements. By the time of the church's formal beginning in 1830, ten years had passed since Mormonism's founder, Joseph Smith, had had the first of many visions upon which the faith—then and now—rests. Joseph Smith and his family, farmers in the newly settled town of Palmyra in upstate New York, had been spiritually stirred by the preaching of revivalist Protestant ministers seeking souls in the area.

In a guileless attempt, like Luther, to answer troubling personal questions (which church is right? and how can I be saved?) Joseph determined in the spring of 1820 when not yet fifteen years of age to follow the counsel of the Apostle James in the Bible. "If any of you lack wisdom," this ancient disciple of Christ had written, "let him ask of God, that giveth to all men liberally, and upbraideth not; and it shall be given him." (James 1:5) Joseph described later the impact this advice had on him: "Never did any passage of scripture come with more power to the heart of man than this did at this time to mine. It seemed to enter with great force into every feeling of my heart. I reflected on it again and again, knowing that if any person needed wisdom from God, I did." (Smith, *History* 1:12)

The result was a majestic vision—the first of many during the next twenty-four years—where as Joseph Smith recounted later, God, the Father, and Jesus Christ appeared to him. They assured him of his worthiness before them, told him to join none of the churches, and promised to "restore" the original church of Christ. When Joseph recounted the incident to his family, his younger brother, William, later recalled

. . . The whole family were melted to tears, and believed all he said. Knowing that

Opposite left: A small boy stands on the spot where Mormons believe Joseph Smith on a sunny spring morning in 1820 was visited by God The Father and His Son, Jesus Christ. (Photo by George Edward Anderson, 1908)

he was very young, that he had not enjoyed the advantages of a common education; and knowing, too, his whole character and disposition, they were convinced that he was totally incapable of arising before his aged parents, his brothers and sisters, and so solemnly giving utterance to anything but the truth. (Quoted in Arrington and Bitton, 3)

What had begun as a personal quest became, however, an event of such "vast historical importance," as historian Richard Bushman described it, that it overshadowed the strictly personal significance. "A new era in history began at that moment. Joseph's personal salvation paled in comparison to the fact that the God of Heaven had set His hand again to open a new dispensation." (Bushman, 57)

What had begun was the unfolding of a new religion, with answers to many of what an American intellectual historian, Franklin Baumer, has called the "perennial" questions of life, "the deepest questions man can ask about himself and his universe"; "Does God exist? How do we know he exists? and if he exists, what are his attributes? What is man? Does [he] have a fixed nature, or is he malleable, like soft wax or clay, conditioned, possibly even determined, by his environment?" (Baumer, 14) These and many other similar questions about nature, freedom, history, and society, thoughtful people wrestle with and seek answers to as part of the uniquely human condition.

Gradually throughout the 1830s and early 40s Joseph Smith gave Mormonism's answers to these and other questions. These answers have satisfied and given meaning to the lives of the stream of seekers who have come into contact with members and missionaries. Most converts also received some kind of spiritual manifestation that confirmed their faith and became a primary motivation for lives of sacrifice and service.

Joseph's later visions, beginning in 1827, led to the bringing forth of the Book of Mormon, a book of sacred scripture written on gold plates that were buried nearby in the Hill Cumorah and were given him by a divine messenger, Moroni, himself an earlier prophet among the peoples described in the book. Eleven other men, friends of the Smiths, testified that they saw or felt the plates, while enemies gave their own indirect testimony to their existence by trying to steal them. The book was, Moroni told Joseph Smith, a record of God's dealings with people who had lived before and after Christ in the western hemisphere. As in ancient Israel, they, too, had had prophets who brought them God's word and were visited by the resurrected Jesus Christ with his message and hope. Their civilizations had eventually disappeared because of sin and strife, and their records had been lost until the Book of Mormon was presented for public consideration in March, 1830. Joseph Smith and his scribe, Oliver Cowdery, had translated this 584-page text—a Herculean task—during the months of April, May, and June, 1829. The book was intended to be—and has been to believers—a second witness, along with the Bible, for the existence of God and the divinity of Jesus Christ and his message. Mormons have found it difficult to comprehend that some traditional Christians thought they were not "Christians." In the nineteenth century non-Mormons used Mormon peculiarity as a basis for a variety of forms of persecution and ostracism; for Mormons it became a badge of courage but also a source of alienation and opposition. It is certainly true, as has been noted, that Mormon doctrines departed from the canon of faith accepted by the established churches; but that is, indeed, what has made it a "new faith" and a "new religion." And while it departs in doc-

trine, organization and practice from some traditional Christian norms, in its fundamentals, Mormonism is quintessentially Christian.

As evidence of their fundamental commitment to Christ, Mormons point to their real name (Church of Jesus Christ of Latter-day Saints) which they believe was divinely given; to their central belief in the divine Sonship of Jesus Christ, the literal son of God and the author of salvation, to the confirming testimony of the Book of Mormon as well as other latter-day revelations; and to their belief that Christ is *the* exemplar for how life should be lived. They believe literally and completely in the declaration of the Apostle Peter that Christ was bodily resurrected from the dead and that ". . . there is none other name under heaven given among men, whereby we must be saved." (Acts 4:12)

Understandably, there have been from the beginning critics of Joseph, of the faith, and of the origins and validity of Book of Mormon. Some neighbors thought Joseph a money-digger and a shiftless young man; Joseph's father-in-law, Isaac Hale, was not enthusiastic about the curious young man his daughter, Emma, had married. Not only did his story sound like a fantastic tale, but the emergence of new "scripture"—a "Gold Bible" —alongside the real Bible was viewed by many as a form of Mormon blasphemy. Still, no other explanation of the book's existence, not even the oft-repeated Spaulding Manuscript theory, has attained enduring credibility. In addition, the whole notion of continuous divine revelation, both for the prophets and the people, a fundamental Mor-

Farms surround the Hill Cumorah before the turn of the twentieth century. This view is much as it would have been in Joseph Smith's time, when he received the plates of the Book of Mormon. (John F. Bennett Collection, Utah Historical Society)

mon belief then and now, is intimately tied to the Book of Mormon experience. Brigham Young, the second Mormon president, had said in his uniquely colorful language that he would not give "the ashes of a rye straw" (quoted in Cowley, 226) for a church that did not have such ongoing direction from God. But the book and how it came about violated the doctrines of established Christianity and became a major cause of persecution, mostly from devout and well-meaning Christian believers, unhappily a dominant feature of the earlier nineteenth century Mormon historic experience.

For Mormons, the Book of Mormon was and has remained a treasure-trove of divine wisdom and a primary source of individual spiritual experience. Typical is the account in 1848 by Orson Spencer, a former Baptist clergyman who was graduated from Hamilton Literary and Theological College in 1829 and became in 1850 one of the church's first missionaries to Prussia, where he spent most of his time in jail. While later serving a mission in England he described his initial experience with the Book of Mormon:

> I arose from its perusal with a strong conviction on my mind, that its pages were graced with the pen of inspiration. I was surprised that so little fault could be found with a book of such magnitude, treating, as it did, of such diversified subjects, through a period of so many generations. It appeared to me that no enemy to truth or godliness would ever take the least interest in publishing the contents of such a book; such appeared to me its godly bearing, sound morality, and harmony with ancient scriptures, that the enemy of all righteousness might as well proclaim the dissolution of his own kingdom, as to spread the contents of such a volume among men; and from that time to this, every effort made by its enemies to demolish [it], has only shown how invincible a fortress defends it . . . On this subject I only ask the friends of pure religion to read the Book of Mormon with the same unprejudiced, prayerful, and teachable spirit that they would recommend unbelievers in the ancient scriptures to read those sacred records. (Spencer, 10–11)

For the current President of the Church, Ezra Taft Benson, the Book of Mormon remains "the cornerstone of our religion." Each Mormon believes that he, too, can know for himself through study and spiritual means that the Book of Mormon is a true record and that Joseph Smith, its translator, was God's prophet for this age.

But Mormonism even in 1830 was more than just a book and an unfolding theology. It was power and organization to spread the word and organize and purify the believers. In 1829, Joseph Smith and Oliver Cowdery, his scribe and friend, recorded visitations by other heavenly beings, especially the ancient apostles Peter, James, and John, who conferred on them "priesthood authority," divine power to organize and "restore" the church and carry out the ordinances of salvation, such as baptism and the laying on of hands, for the gift of the Holy Ghost as well as practice the spiritual gifts as Jesus and his apostles had done. All of these, Mormons believe, were prerequisites for the "restoration" of the original church of Christ that spring day in 1830.

From the beginning the Church of Jesus Christ of Latter-day Saints, like the early Christian Church, has been a proselyting church. The message of the restoration was not just for the heathen and the unchurched, but "for every kindred, tongue, and

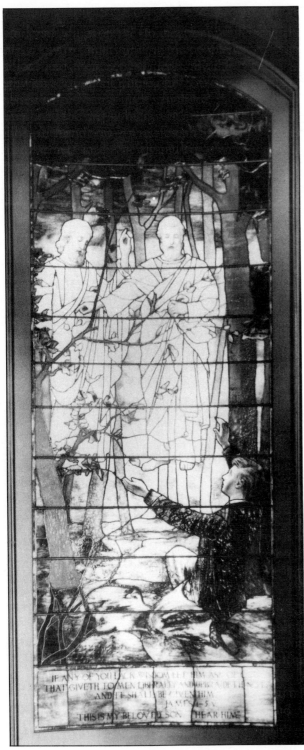

A stained glass window in the Mormon Temple in Salt Lake City depicts the heavenly visitation to Joseph Smith in the Sacred Grove in Palmyra, New York. (Photo by Ralph Savage, 1912)

people." To Mormons this meant bringing their message to all peoples of the world. From the days when the first missionary, Samuel Smith, Joseph's younger brother, tramped the backroads of New York and New England and asked people such as Brigham Young and Heber C. Kimball, later Mormon stalwarts, to read the Book of Mormon and consider the new faith, an estimated 350,000 missionaries have crisscrossed the cities and hamlets of North and South America, Western Europe, Oceania, and parts of Asia and Africa to explain the message to all who would listen. A revelation given to Joseph Smith in June 1829 before the church was organized, established the enduring importance of missionary work:

> Remember the worth of souls is great in the sight of God . . . Wherefore, you are called to cry repentance unto this people. And if it so be that you should labor all your days in crying repentance unto this people, and bring save it be one soul unto me, how great shall be your joy with him in the kingdom of my Father.

> And now, if your joy will be great with one soul that you have brought unto me into the kingdom of my Father, how great will be your joy if you shall bring many souls unto me. (Doctrine & Covenants 18:10, 14–16)

Two years later another revelation gave clearer definition of what the missionaries and their converts were to do:

> Go ye out of Babylon; gather ye out from among the nations, from the four winds, from one end of heaven to the other.

> Send forth the elders of my church unto the nations which are afar off; unto the islands of the sea; send forth unto foreign lands; call upon all nations, first upon the Gentiles, and then upon the Jews. (Doctrine & Covenants 133: 7–8)

Throughout Mormon history, missionaries lived either from the care of members and friends or from their own or family's money. Missionary work was always hard; virtually no one would do it for any other cause. Sometimes missionaries would feel the discouragement and bitterness of an Orson Hyde, an early apostle-missionary in the United States, in Europe in the 1840s, and later in Palestine:

I felt that all my old friends [not of the Mormons] would believe me, and with a warm and affectionate heart, I soon went out among them, and began to talk and testify to them what the Lord had done for me; but the cold indifference with which they received me, and the pity they expressed for my delusion, soon convinced me that it was not wise to give that which is holy unto dogs, neither to cast pearls before swine. ("History of Brigham Young")

Usually the reward came in the supreme joy of finding one soul looking for what the missionaries had; occasionally, hundreds would request baptism at one time as was the case with Wilford Woodruff, Heber C. Kimball, or Dan Jones in England and Wales in the early 1840s. Mary Ann Weston Maughan, a later pioneer who helped build the Mormon West, recalled how the storied Woodruff brought Mormonism to her in Herefordshire:

Soon Brother Woodruff came to our house. There was no one at home but me. He sat by the fire and soon commenced singing . . . Brother Jenkins [with whom she boarded] told us that he had left his home in America, crossed the sea and [had] come to preach this gospel to the people in England. While he was singing I looked at him. He was so peaceful and happy I thought he must be a good man and the gospel he preached must be true. (Quoted in Godfrey et al., 35–36)

Today, more than 35,000 young men and women and a few older couples volunteer two years of their time and talents at their own expense to share their faith in virtually all parts of the world. The missionary work continues; it is the life blood of Mormonism.

A map of New England shows the roots of the Mormon Church, from the mountains of Vermont, to the Finger Lakes of upstate New York, to the Susquehanna River region of Pennsylvania.

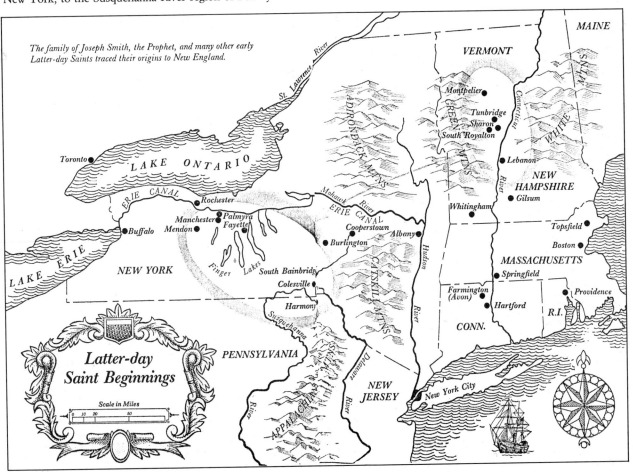

The family of Joseph Smith, the Prophet, and many other early Latter-day Saints traced their origins to New England.

Latter-day Saint Beginnings

Scale in Miles

The Smith family home near Palmyra, New York, has been restored and kept in its pristine condition by the Mormon Church. The Smiths lived here from 1824 to 1830, a most crucial period in the development of Mormonism. (Photo by George Edward Anderson, 1908)

Two Mormon missionaries visit the room in the Smith home near Palmyra, New York, where Joseph Smith said he was visited by a heavenly messenger named Angel Moroni. Mormons believe the angel led Joseph Smith to the gold plates of the Book of Mormon. (Photo by George D. Parkinson while on mission to New York, 1904)

Right: A buggy winds its way over the dirt road in front of the Hill Cumorah in 1908 and stops for the lone occupant to have his picture taken with the historic Mormon hill in the background. (Photo by George Edward Anderson, 1908)

Above: Children play o[n] country lane leading to [the] Sacred Grove in New Y[ork]. Joseph Smith walked down [the] lane in the spring of 182[0 to] pray in the grove's peace[ful] solitude. (Photo by Ge[orge] Edward Anderson, 1908)

Opposite right: A horse-dr[awn] sled transports a storage t[ank] for maple sugar through sta[nds] of maple trees near Palm[yra,] New York. (Photo by Ge[orge] Edward Anderson, 1908)

Left: Workers harvest sap f[rom] maple sugar trees that surro[und] the Smith farm near Palm[yra,] New York. (Photo by Ge[orge] Edward Anderson, 1908)

Left: A steel engraving shows the three witnesses who signed le
documents testifying that Angel Moroni had also appeared to th
to let them see the golden plates of the Book of Mormon. They
Oliver Cowdery, David Whitmer, and Martin Harris. They ne
denied their testimonies. (John F. Bennett Collection, Utah Hist
ical Society)

Opposite right: A gold box in the Utah State University Library
Logan contains a first edition of the Book of Mormon owned
former USU President Daryl Chase. The receptacle for the valua
book was a gift from the Iranian alumni of the university bef
Chase's retirement. An inscription on the inside lid says, "To th
beloved President Daryl Chase with heartfelt wishes and sentim
of deep respect ..." (Special Collections, Utah State Univers
Library)

Below: A fragment of characters copied from the Book of Mormon plates and submitted for authentication to professors in New York C
show unusual Old-World hieroglyphics. (Utah State University Library)

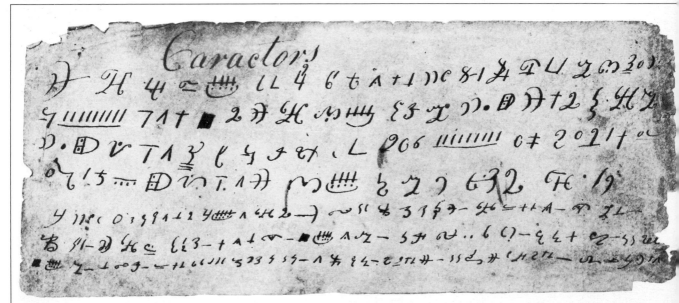

THE
BOOK OF MORMON:

AN ACCOUNT WRITTEN BY THE HAND OF MOR
MON, UPON PLATES TAKEN FROM
THE PLATES OF NEPHI

BY JOSEPH SMITH, JUNIOR,
AUTHOR AND PROPRIETOR.

PALMYRA:
PRINTED BY E. B. GRANDIN, FOR THE AUTHOR.
1830.

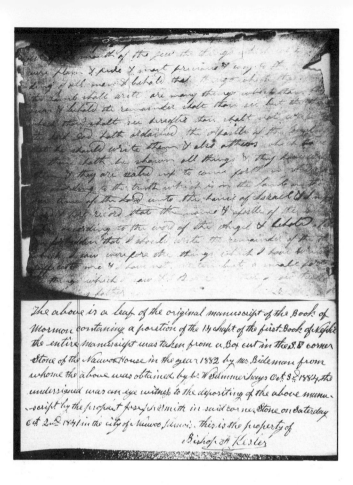

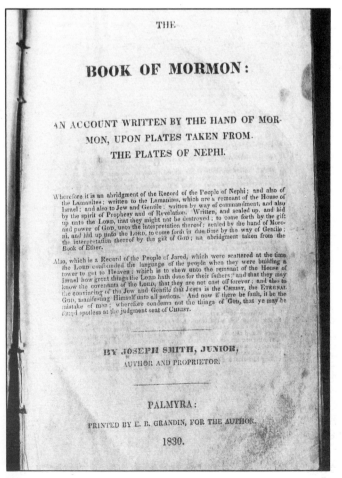

Above: A dirt main street fronts the building where the Bo[ok] Mormon was first published in Palmyra, New York, in 1830. (P[hoto] by George Edward Anderson, 1908)

Above left: Among the H. Kesler papers at the University of [Utah] are this leaf from the original manuscript of the Book of Mo[rmon] in Oliver Cowdery's handwriting. The writing is a portion of Ch[apter] 14, First Book of Nephi. Attached to it is an "eye witness" state[ment] from Bishop Kesler explaining how the leaf was initially depo[sited] in the cornerstone of the Nauvoo House by Joseph Smith in [1841] (for a daguerreotype portrait of Bishop Kesler, see page 33). (W[est-] ern Americana Collection, University of Utah)

Lower left: The title page of the Book of Mormon explains [from] where the ancient records came and to whom they are writte[n:] "to the convincing of Jew and Gentile that Jesus is the Chris[t, the] Eternal God, manifesting Himself unto all nations." (From a[n 1830] edition in the Utah State University Library Special Collectio[ns])

w: A granite craftsman works on a section of the Joseph Smith [Mon]ument, which memorializes publication of the Book of Mormon [in Pa]lmyra, New York, in 1830. (Mormon Church Historical De[part]ment)

Below: Upstairs, above the M. Story Dry Goods Co., was Egbert B. Grandin's *Wayne Sentinel* newspaper and printing establishment where the Book of Mormon first edition was published. (Photo by George Edward Anderson, 1908)

Martin Harris, who played a key role in publication of the Book of Mormon and in early Church history, is photographed in Utah shortly before his death in 1875. (Mormon Church Historical Department)

Modern railroad tracks pass in front of the Martin Harris farm near Palmyra, New York, when photographed by George Edward Anderson in 1908. Harris mortgaged his farm to raise the money to print the Book of Mormon. (Photo by George Edward Anderson, 1908)

A ram grazes on the Smith farm in Manchester, New York, where the roots of the Mormon Church were first established by Joseph Smith after publication of the Book of Mormon. Early baptisms were held in this small stream. (Photo by George Edward Anderson, 1908)

Right: Boats ply the Susquehanna River near the spot where Mormons believe Joseph Smith and Oliver Cowdery were visited by John the Baptist and received the keys to restore the Aaronic Priesthood. The two men baptized each other in the river. (Photo by George Edward Anderson)

An old man makes his way down the lane in front of the Isaac Hale home in Harmony, Pennsylvania, where Joseph Smith and Oliver Cowdery lived while translating much of the Book of Mormon. The home was still standing in 1908 when photographed by George Edward Anderson. (Photo by George Edward Anderson)

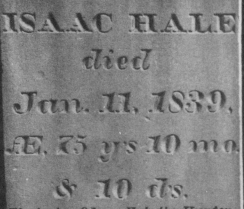

ISAAC HALE
died
Jan. 11, 1839,
Æ. 75 yrs 10 mo.
& 10 ds.
The body of Isaac Hale, the Hunter,
like the cover of an old book, its contents
torn out, and stript of its lettering and
guilding, lies here food for worms, yet the
work itself shall not be lost for it will
as he believed appear once more in
a new and more beautiful edition,
corrected and amended.

TOMBSTONE'S
FATHER AND MOTHER IN
OF JOSEPH SMITH (THE
MCKUNE CEMETRY NEAR

Left: The tombstones of Isaac and Elizabeth Hale, father- and mother-in-law of Joseph Smith, can be found in the McKune Cemetery near Susquehanna, Pennsylvania. Isaac Hale died in 1839 and his wife in 1842, before the Mormon prophet's martyrdom. (Photo by George Edward Anderson, 1907)

Overleaf, pages 70 and 71: Emma Hale, daughter of Isaac Hale of Harmony, Pennsylvania, married Joseph Smith, Jr., in 1827. The view on page 70 is believed to be executed from a daguerreotype by painter William Majors in 1844. The photograph on page 71 was taken by an unknown photographer later in her life in Nauvoo, after the main body of the Mormon Church accepted Brigham Young as their leader and migrated west to the Utah Territory. (Mormon Church Historical Department)

Overleaf, pages 72–73: An old lithograph depicts Joseph Smith preaching to the Indians on the western frontier in the early 1830s. Mormons believe the Book of Mormon contains a history of early America, including origins of the Indians. (Mormon Church Historical Department)

Below: A tombstone in Harmony, Pennsylvania, marks the grave of an infant son of Joseph and Emma Smith. Don Carlos Smith, aged 14 months, died June 15, 1829. (Photo by George Edward Anderson)

KIRTLAND, OHIO.

OHIO AND MISSOURI

By 1831 enough animosity had emerged in New York for Joseph Smith to move his small congregation westward to Kirtland, near Cleveland, Ohio, where missionaries such as Oliver Cowdery the year before had found numerous sympathetic converts. It was the beginning of a period of Mormon wandering in America reminiscent of ancient Israel, with whom early Mormons identified. At about the same time a second center was founded in western Missouri, near present-day Kansas City, a place where Mormons thought they would build the biblical New Jerusalem, but it was not to be. In both places Joseph continued to receive revelations; the fullness of the Christian Gospel was being revealed.

In Kirtland, the first Mormon "temple," a sanctuary not unlike those of ancient Israel where special ceremonies and rites were performed, was established at great cost ($60,000) to the Saints. It became a sacred spot where revelations were received and spiritual gifts manifested. Here, for example, Joseph gazed into eternity and learned of God's plan of salvation for all of his children. The hereafter was not a simple heaven or hell, but varying degrees of heaven; a person's reward was based on how well he kept the commandments in this life. God, Joseph discovered, was indeed just and merciful.

At the same time, internal dissension rocked the foundation of the church in Ohio with several prominent leaders, such as David Whitmer and Oliver Cowdery, leaving the church because of differences with Joseph over land purchases and other financial matters. Joseph countered the difficulties in 1837 by sending Heber C. Kimball and several other missionaries to begin their successful preaching mission to the people of Great Britain. Kimball stepped ashore as Queen Victoria began her long

Opposite left: Kirtland, Ohio, was among the first Mormon settlements on the western frontier. Converts to the fast-growing church began settling here in 1831. In the foreground, left, is the cemetery adjacent to the Mormon Temple. (Mormon Church Historical Department)

Below: A bank bill of the Kirtland Safety Society, signed by Joseph Smith, illustrates a brief but disastrous experiment in banking during the Mormons' stay in Ohio. Because the state would not grant the bank a charter, its currency was not recognized by other banks and the venture ended in failure. (Utah Historical Society)

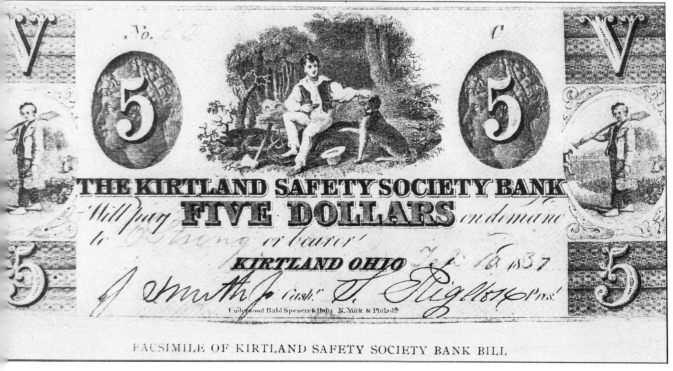

FACSIMILE OF KIRTLAND SAFETY SOCIETY BANK BILL

reign, and launched what became an incredible success story. By 1850, the Mormon community in Britain numbered more than 30,000, not including several hundred who had already begun the massive and well-organized Mormon emigration first to Nauvoo, Illinois and then to Utah, that would eventually bring before 1900 an estimated 85,000 Europeans—overwhelmingly laborers, miners, farmers, and artisans—from Britain, Scandinavia, Switzerland, and Germany to build up the Mormon Kingdom. Mormons called it the "gathering to Zion." A contemporary historian, Katherine Coman, described it as "the most successful example of regulated immigration in United States history." (Quoted in Poll et al., 185)

By 1838 there were an estimated 7,000 Mormons in Missouri, but experiences there were worse than they had been in Ohio. Some Mormons who had migrated there were overbearing and arrogant; God, they claimed, had given them this land to be the center of the new Kingdom in preparation for Christ's second coming. Missouri was a frontier that had attracted the rougher elements of early America; these people felt threatened by the organized invasion of a new large homogenous religious group. What followed was the most severe persecution the Mormons had yet known. Mobs bent on murder, massacres, and marauding drove Mormons from one Missouri county to another. Mormons were, for their part, accused of having instigated the violence. Joseph Smith and friends were held in inhuman jails for months at a time, subjected to indignities and cruelty and even threatened with death. Missouri's governor, Lilburn Boggs, proclaimed his infamous Order of Extermination on October 27, 1838. "The Mormons," he wrote to a state militia office, "must be treated as enemies and must be exterminated or driven from the state, if necessary for the public good. Their outrages are beyond all description." (Smith, *History* 3:175) One Mormon woman, Drusilla Hendrichs, recalled those troubled days:

> The summer passed until August [1838] without any trouble. We had had just three years of peace, but the first of August our trouble began over the election. My husband had to stand guard for three months, as the mob would gather on the

The Kirtland Temple was the first built by the Mormons. It was completed in 1836 but abandoned a year later when the Mormons moved to Missouri. (Utah Historical Society)

Above: An old cemetery stands in the foreground of this view of the Kirtland Temple, taken from its backside by Utah photographer George Edward Anderson on visit in 1907. (Photo by George Edward Anderson)

Right: An interior view of the Kirtland Temple shows the arrangement of seats and its unique front altars. (Utah Historical Society)

outside settlement. The brethren had to be ready and on hand at the sounding of a brass drum. At three taps on the drum my husband would be on his horse in a moment, be it night or day, while I and my children were left to weep, for that is what we did at such times. (Quoted in Godfrey et al., 89)

But Missouri, like Ohio, was not all trial and tribulation for the Mormons. Here Joseph received some of the most profound and sublime revelations of his life, revelations that Mormons—and non-Mormons who have considered them—cherish to this day. Two examples are illustrative. In 1838, Joseph received a revelation establishing the "law of tithing," which has remained for over a century the principal source of funding for the church as well as a barometer of worthiness. One tenth of each Mormon's gross income is given as a tithe to God. Presently, an estimated 20 to 30 percent of church members pay a full tithe. A year later while in jail, at Liberty, Missouri, Joseph gained profound insights into the proper use of power, especially God's priesthood power, from which millions of Mormons have benefited.

No power or influence can or ought to be maintained by virtue of the priesthood, only by persuasion, by long-suffering, by gentleness and meekness, and by love un-feigned.

By kindness and pure knowledge which shall greatly enlarge the soul without hypocrisy, and without guile.

Reproving betimes with sharpness when moved upon by the Holy Ghost; and then showing forth afterwards an increase of love toward him whom thou hast reproved, lest he esteem thee to be his enemy.

That he may know that thy faithfulness is stronger than the cords of death. (Doctrine & Covenants 121:41–44)

A band of Missouri militia raids the Mormon settlement of Haun's Mill, killing men, women, and children. The Haun's Mill Massacre was the beginning of a wave of persecutions that culminated in the expulsion of the Latter-day Saints from the state of Missouri. (Old woodcut, Brigham Young University archives)

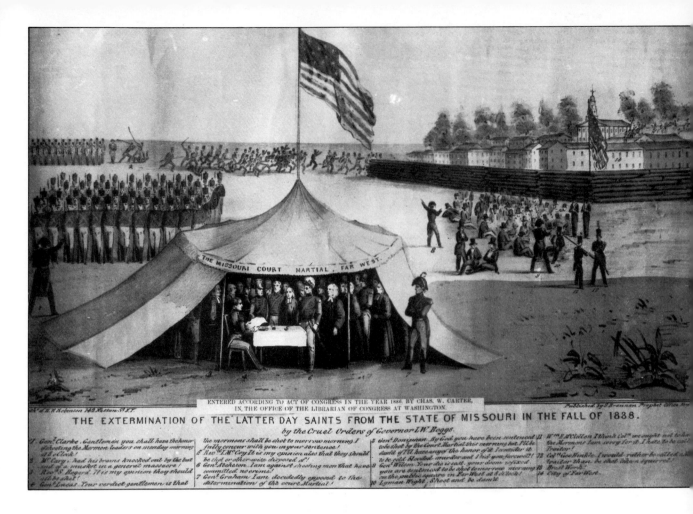

THE EXTERMINATION OF THE LATTER DAY SAINTS FROM THE STATE OF MISSOURI IN THE FALL OF 1838.
by the Cruel Orders of Governor L.W. Boggs.

Above: A sketch published in Sam Brannan's newspaper, *The Prop* in New York depicts the surrender of the Mormons at Far W Missouri, after Governor Boggs had issued orders to his militia the Mormons should either be exterminated or driven from the s in the fall of 1838. (Mormon Church Historical Department)

Opposite right, top: The Temple Lot in Independence, Misso stands vacant when photographed in 1890. Mormons had lai cornerstone for a temple here in 1831 but the building never off the ground. Mormons still believe a temple will one day rise this site. (Mormon Church Historical Department)

Opposite right, bottom: An old albumen print shows a general s in Kirtland after the Mormons had left. The Latter-day Saints cupied Kirtland between 1831 and 1837, before the advent of p tography. (Mormon Church Historical Department)

Left: Sidney Rigdon, shown here in an old lithograph, served in Mormon Church's First Presidency from 1833 to 1844. Altho one of the strong leaders in the early years, Rigdon eventually Mormonism after he was not chosen to succeed Joseph Smit president of the Mormon Church after Smith's murder. (Ben Collection, Utah Historical Society)

Above: An old millstone is all that is left of the Haun's Mill settlement in Missouri, where 17 Mormons were massacred by a mob in 1838, when photographer George Edward Anderson makes this view in 1907. "At Haun's Mill," Anderson wrote in his diary, "crossed the creek and located left of the old mill, stones which we worked out of the ground and down to the edge of the creek. Made two or three negatives of it, putting an inscription on one side. Mr. Parker H. Elmer, Levi Nichols, furnished the paint and brush." (Photo by George Edward Anderson, May 23, 1907)

The church also continued to grow so that, even after the bloodshed and the flight out of Missouri in 1839, from the sixty-two members at the beginning of the decade, a respectable following of nearly 30,000 throughout the United States and Britain had emerged.

Left: Shoal Creek winds its way through Caldwell County, Missouri, the site of the Haun's Mill Massacre. The mill was situated on the creek, just across the water from the boy standing on the bank in the center of this photograph. (Photo by George Edward Anderson, 1907)

Overleaf, pages 84–85: Andrew Jenson, Joseph S. Black, and Edward Stevenson visit the Liberty Jail in Missouri in 1892. The jail is significant in Mormon history because Joseph Smith and other Church leaders were imprisoned here for six months in the winter of 1838–1839. (Mormon Church Historical Department)

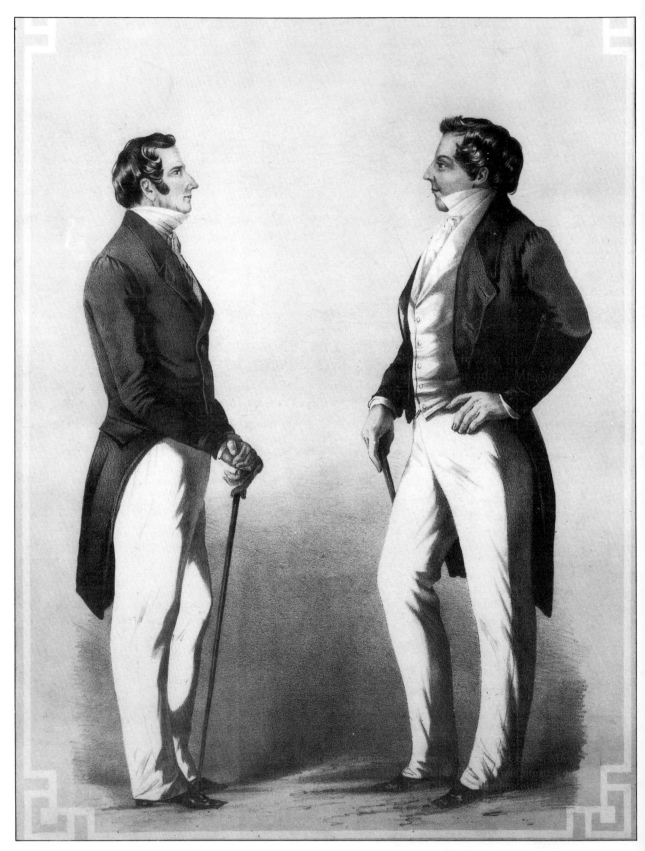

A lithograph by Sarony & Major of New York shows "The Two Martyrs," Hyrum and Joseph Smith. Some believe this was engraved from a photograph. Others believe it is nothing more than an extension of the old Maudsley caricature. (Brigham Young University Archives)

NAUVOO

Forced out of Missouri, Mormon settlers headed east in search of a new place to settle, "... in the most safe and quiet places they can find," Joseph Smith wrote (Smith, *History* 3:301). After some exploration, adequate land was found in western Illinois and eastern Iowa, on either side of the Mississippi River. Mormons called the main settlement in Nauvoo, Illinois, the "Beautiful." In all, they settled at least nineteen different townsites in Illinois alone.

Nauvoo looked like the long-sought refuge for the growing church. Land was purchased, solid brick homes constructed, businesses established, and erection of a new temple begun on a hill overlooking the city. City leaders obtained a charter from the government of Illinois giving Mormons the political power to govern their own affairs and, if possible, preclude the violence that had plagued them elsewhere in the preceding decade. They even formed the Nauvoo Legion, a city militia designed to offer security from mobs that might develop. Prospects looked bright, indeed, and by the early 1840s Nauvoo enjoyed a remarkable prosperity.

Not a small part of that prosperity derived from the arrival in 1840 of the first European Mormon immigrants, a group of forty English Saints. By the end of the Nauvoo era, some 4,733 British Mormons, mostly artisans and laboring people, had

A seemingly deserted Nauvoo glimmers in the afternoon light in this 1846 daguerreotype believed to be taken by Lucian Foster. The completed temple sits atop the hill, overlooking the city. The photo was copied from the original daguerreotype by Charles William Carter in Salt Lake City but it has since been lost. Only the copy negative remains. (Mormon Church Historical Department)

come in order to avoid the judgments they believed God was sending upon a wicked world—Babylon—in the last days, and to be part of the rise of the new Zion. Thousands of Britons had become Mormons since the beginning of the missionary work there, but especially during and following the mission of 1840–1841 when a majority of the members of the Quorum of the Twelve Apostles, including most of the greatest church leaders in the nineteenth century, not just Kimball and Woodruff but Brigham Young, John Taylor, Parley P. Pratt and his brother, Orson, and George A. Smith, labored there with great success.

When the missionary apostles arrived in January, 1840 some 1500 Saints lived in Great Britain; when they left fifteen months later, there were 5,814 members—and another 800 had emigrated to America. But these zealous preachers accomplished other things that would characterize Mormon proselyting for more than a century. In addition to printing 5,000 copies of the *Book of Mormon* and a lesser number of a hymnal, they began a periodical, *The Latter-Day Saints' Millennial Star*, the mouthpiece for the church in Europe for more than 130 years, and also missionary tracts on a wide variety of subjects. Missionaries now had much better tools with which to present their message.

A caricature of Lt. Gen. Joseph Smith, the Mormon Prophet, was drawn by English designer Sutcliff Maudsley, creating a flat, side view that would be the basis of Smith's visual image for many years. (Mormon Church Historical Department)

The short Nauvoo experience—1839–1846—began in hope and expectation and ended in tragedy and flight. By the time of the mob murder of Joseph and Hyrum Smith in June of 1844, in neighboring Carthage, not only had a beautiful and prosperous city been built on original Mississippi swamplands by a people of energy, purpose, and faith, but also the unique theology of the Latter-day Saints begun in New York and expanded in Ohio and Missouri was essentially rounded out. When forced to flee toward the American West, Mormons had already received through their prophet the "fullness of the Gospel," all of the doctrines, ordinances, and powers necessary for salvation.

Before his death, Joseph Smith had been asked by a Chicago newspaper editor, John Wentworth, to articulate in summary form the church's beliefs. While not a complete survey of Mormon theology, these "Articles of Faith" are still revered by Latter-day Saints as a credo, an expression of their basic beliefs. They are as follows:

1. We believe in God, the Eternal Father, and in His Son Jesus Christ, and in the Holy Ghost.
2. We believe that men will be punished for their own sins, and not for Adam's transgression.
3. We believe that through the Atonement of Christ, all mankind may be saved, by obedience to the laws and ordinances of the Gospel.
4. We believe that the first principles and ordinances of the Gospel are: first, Faith in the Lord Jesus Christ; second, Repentance; third, Baptism by immersion for the remission of sins; fourth, Laying on of hands for the gift of the Holy Ghost.
5. We believe that a man must be called

A painting found in the possessions of Joseph Smith's wife, Emma, by the late Mormon memorabilia collector Wilford Wood of Woods Cross, Utah. Scholars disagree on whether a photograph from life was ever taken of Joseph Smith, but the visual images seem to suggest a common source, possibly a daguerreotype taken by daguerreotypist Lucian Foster of New York, a friend of the Mormon prophet who advertised daguerreotyping services in Nauvoo in August of 1844, less than three months after Joseph Smith's death.

Nauvoo is also pictured from Montrose by Frederick Hawkins Piercy, who sketched the deserted city in 1853 on his way to the Great Salt Lake Valley with a company of emigrants from England. Piercy's drawings are quite accurate because he "used a *camera lucida* to make sketches from life." (Copied from Piercy's *Route from Liverpool to Great Salt Lake Valley*)

of God, by prophecy, and by the laying on of hands by those who are in authority, to preach the Gospel and administer in the ordinances thereof.

6. We believe in the same organization that existed in the Primitive Church, namely, apostles, prophets, pastors, teacher, evangelists, and so forth.

7. We believe in the gift of tongues, prophecy, revelation, visions, healing, interpretation of tongues, and so forth.

8. We believe the Bible to be the word of God, as far as it is translated correctly; we also believe the Book of Mormon to be the word of God.

9. We believe all that God has revealed, all that He does now reveal, and we believe He will yet reveal, many great and important things pertaining to the Kingdom of God.

10. We believe in the literal gathering of Israel and in the restoration of the Ten Tribes; that Zion (the New Jerusalem) will be built upon the American continent; that Christ will reign personally upon the earth; and, that the earth will be renewed and receive its paradisiacal glory.

11. We claim the privilege of worshipping Almighty God according to the dictates of our own conscience, and allow all men the same privilege, let them worship how, where, or what they may.

12. We believe in being subject to kings, presidents, rulers, and magistrates, in obeying, honoring and sustaining the law.

13. We believe in being honest, true, chaste, benevolent, virtuous, and in doing good to all men; indeed, we may say that we follow the admonition of Paul—We believe all things, we hope all things, we have endured many things, and we hope to be able to endure all things. If there is anything virtuous, lovely, or of good report or praiseworthy, we seek after these things. (Smith, *History* 4:535–541)

The Nauvoo House, which next to the Temple was to be the most pretentious building in Nauvoo, is situated at the end of Main Street. The building was never completed as planned, but other structures were built on its foundation, as this old photograph shows. (Mormon Church Historical Department)

In Nauvoo, Joseph Smith reached the pinnacle of respect and power among the Mormons as God's prophet, seer, and revelator. He was revered like Moses, Isaiah, Peter, and Paul, and his successors have been similarly viewed. Throughout their history Mormons have carved a special niche in their

The Joseph Smith Homestead in Nauvoo, Illinois, was the first dwelling of the Mormon prophet when he settled in the fledgling city in 1839. (Brigham Young University Archives)

affections for those men who have been called to reveal God's word to the church as a whole. They still believe for each what Joseph said of himself, "I never told you I was perfect, but there is no error in the revelations which I have taught you." (Smith, *Teachings*, 368)

One member who joined the church in 1843 in Nauvoo was Dan Jones, a native Welshman, who later became a boat captain on the Mississippi River. Jones has left a vivid account of his conversion and his first meeting of Joseph Smith:

In spite of my conversion, somehow I had not one particle of love for old "Joe Smith." I could swallow almost everything except his being a prophet of God. For as long as I could remember, I had formed some strange ideas as to what kind of men the early prophets were. I thought that they should wear—and consequently "Joe Smith" should wear before he could be a prophet—either a sheep or goat skin, a long beard, and long, white hair, and his face should be long and wrinkled with a high and retiring gaze, murmuring quite a lot and very saintly. I almost thought that he ought to be a wanderer on the mountains without ever coming to a house or to a table, but living on locusts and the like. And when he came among people to deliver his divine message, he would do that in a manner that would prove to everyone that he was a prophet.

While the baseless imaginings like these were contending for space in my mind mixed with the thousand and one false accusations so unfounded which I had heard about that remarkable person, I took my steamboat with over 300 immigrants (Saints) from St. Louis to Nauvoo. When we arrived a large crowd of respectable-looking people came to greet us very hospitable. Such hand-shaking and kissing among the women, and such a "hearty welcome" as they met each other rather surprised me.

Even greater than my surprise was my disappointment when I ran my eyes over the crowd and failed to find anyone similar to the prophet I had pictured. But then a large, comely man came up to me in the crowd on the boat, took my hand and squeezing it kindly, said, "God bless you brother" several times. Before I could ask his name he was out of sight. And then he came by again, at which time I understood that my eyes for the second time beheld Joseph Smith, the Mormon prophet! Although things were busy I took time to study him. And everything I saw in him was contrary to my expectation. His fair countenance and his cheerful, guileless face rather convinced me that he was not the cunning and deceitful man I had heard about. His humility and the wondrous and respectful love which everyone showed him obliged me to believe that this was not the cruel oppressor who considered everyone his slave. Yes, in short, I was soon convinced that much of what I had heard about the man was false accusations.

John Taylor, who was with Joseph Smith in Carthage Jail and was wounded during the shooting, is pictured here in the 1850s while serving as a Mormon apostle in Salt Lake City. He would later become the third president of the Church after the death of Brigham Young. (Photo by Marsena Cannon, 1853. Copied from original daguerreotype)

The home of John Taylor, who would later become the third president of the Mormon Church, was originally built in 1844. Taylor was severely wounded when a mob stormed Carthage Jail and killed Joseph Smith and his brother, Hyrum. (Brigham Young University Archives)

I went with him to his house, and he related to me in a few words a history of more sufferings because of his religion than I had hardly thought possible for anyone to endure so long. Yet he was as certain of his business and as steadfast in his determination as a perpetual rock. He took pride in it all as if he were winning, and before leaving his company I was rather surprised how anyone could doubt that if there ever was a prophet, Joseph Smith was one. (Jones, 59–62)

Jones also came away from the visit with a different view of Nauvoo than what he had heard:

After this I went with him about the city (for it was worthy of the name by then) and I saw everyone about his separate task, looking like everyone else, but more comely and diligent than others. Having circled the place, I failed to observe a drunkard, or a place to get drunk, or an oath or even one useless act! "Could it be," I said, "that everything I heard about this place and this people is false? If not, where is the huge wall which surrounds the city so that no one may come back from it alive?" (as I had heard). There were not two rocks together there for that purpose! Where were all the "slaves" I had heard about, and the business of "all things in common" and many of the other strange things? Everyone here is as free and independent as anyone I ever saw, yes, and each one enjoying his possessions, fruit of his diligence, his family, his money, and his thoughts and his own opinions unhindered. And there was even a state defense for all that freedom. Instead of "Joseph Smith taking others' possessions" or any of the other elders either being supported at the cost of others, as did the "Reverends" and the writers who accused them, they support their families at their own expense.

In this way I got everything to the contrary of what I had heard about the place and its inhabitants, until by the time I

Missionaries and their friends gather for a conference at the Mansion House in Nauvoo, the elegant home of the Mormon prophet at the time of his death in 1844. (Photo by George Edward Anderson)

An old man reads the newspaper in the farm yard of an old home in Nauvoo when George Edward Anderson photographed the city in 1907. (Photo by George Edward Anderson)

arrived back at the boat I was rather ready to say that I would not believe anything from then on about them except what I saw. At least I determined to believe to the contrary of what the Mormons' enemies said about them. And doubtless there were hosts like myself who went there with minds filled with prejudice, and who returned from there with a completely opposite opinion about the place and the people. I saw hosts of such during the time that we were carrying several thousand immigrants there after that. (Ibid.)

Nearly a year later in 1844 Joseph Smith and Nauvoo were visited by two of the most prestigious intellectuals in America: Charles Francis Adams, the son of U.S. President John Quincy Adams; and Josiah Quincy, one year later the Mayor of Boston and the son of a former mayor and President of Harvard College. Quincy has left his impressions. He did not think much of Joseph's theology ("absurdities"), scholarship, or his "bourgeois" tastes, but he was impressed with the man and his city. In 1883 Quincy wrote:

It is by no means improbable that some future textbook, for the use of generations yet unborn, will contain a question something like this: What historical American of the nineteenth century has exerted the most powerful influence upon the destinies of his countrymen? And it is by no means impossible that the answer to that interrogatory may be thus written: Joseph Smith, the Mormon Prophet. And the reply, absurd as it doubtless seems to most men now living, may be an obvious commonplace of their descendants. History deals in surprises and paradoxes quite as startling as this. The man who established a religion in this age of free debate, who was and is today accepted by hundreds of thousands as a direct emissary from the Most High—such a rare human being is not to be disposed of by pelting his memory with unsavory epithets. Fanatic, impostor, charlatan, he may have been; but

A painting by H. Lewis shows a stylized view of the Nauvoo Temple shortly after it was completed in 1845–1846. (Brigham Young University Archives)

these hard names furnish no solution to the problem he presents to us. Fanatics and impostors are living and dying every day, and their memory is buried with them; but the wonderful influence which this founder of a religion exerted and still exerts throws him into relief before us, not as a rogue to be criminated, but as a phenomenon to be explained ... (Mulder and Mortensen, 131–132)

But Joseph also made enemies with some new doctrines he taught. These enemies would eventually organize and incite the mobs that would bring about his death. Man, he explained, was the literal offspring of a God in whose image he had been created. This doctrine, the late Marburg scholar Ernst Benz wrote a few years ago, put Joseph Smith

Opposite left: A rare photograph, copied from a daguerreotype taken in 1845 or 1846, shows how the Nauvoo Temple actually looked when completed. (Mormon Church Historical Department)

Below: One of the 34 hand-hewn sun stones that once adorned the Nauvoo Temple, that capped its pilasters, somehow survived a deliberately set fire. The edifice was burned nearly to the ground in 1846, and the remaining ruins eventually tumbled down. Only a few stones like this one photographed around the turn of the century remained. (Bennett Collection, Utah Historical Society)

and Mormon theology "closer to the view of man of the original Church than the protagonists of the Augustinian doctrine of original sin who considered such a real connection between man and God to be the most fundamental heresy." (Benz, 326)[17] Because of his elevated rather than degraded status, man had freedom of choice and agency and could choose between good and evil. Moreover, all men, Joseph revealed, had lived in a pre-mortal existence and would, through Christ, gain immortality but not necessarily eternal life with God.

Joseph also taught the unique doctrine of salvation for the dead as well as the living. According to this teaching all who have died without having had an opportunity to hear and accept the "fullness of the Gospel" while living on earth, will hear it in the afterlife. But the saving ordinances, including baptism, must be performed here in this life. This doctrine gave some meaning to Paul's enigmatic text in I Corinthians 15:29: "Else what shall they do which are baptized for the dead if the dead rise not at all. Why are they then baptized for the dead?" For this and other purposes, temples such as the one at Nauvoo and subsequent ones in Utah and around the world were—and are—built where these ordinances may be performed by proxy for those who are dead. For this reason beleaguered Mormons in Nauvoo following the death of Joseph Smith worked night and day to finish the temple and gain the blessings they believed could come from the rites performed in it, even though they were already contemplating leaving the city in search of a new home. Brigham Young stated the view of the faithful succinctly: "I would rather pay out every cent to build up this place and receive an endowment, even were I driven the next minute without anything to take with me." (Quoted in Cowley, 227) This doctrine is also the basis for the worldwide Mormon commitment to genealogical research, to a contemporary program of microfilming in some forty countries and the establishment of the largest repository of genealogical records in the world, a collection of names of 1.5 billion people. All of this in order to establish the identity of those for whom these sacred ordinances are to be performed. Temples are thus as much a key to an understanding of Mormon Christianity as they were to ancient Israel.

More controversial then—and especially later —was the doctrine of plural marriage or polygamy

that Joseph revealed in Nauvoo and taught secretly to a few of his closest associates. Plural marriage was not, however, openly preached until 1852 after the Mormons were settled in the relative seclusion of the Salt Lake Valley and then only in America.

Though practiced by Old Testament prophets, polygamy was scorned as a sinful and uncivilized practice by traditional Christians in Europe and America. After getting wind of it for the first time in 1853, the *Times* in London called it a "monstrous heresy" and a "social vice." (Quoted in Lively, 218) Similarly, following a visit with Brigham Young, the noted New York editor Horace Greeley called Mormonism dominated by polygamy "a delusion and a blight." (Arrington, 6) Joseph Smith taught that God had revealed to him that worthy Latter-day Saint men were again to take plural wives for God's own purposes. Polygamy became an accepted Mormon doctrine and was subsequently practiced by a minority of Mormon men until forbidden by law in the United States and discontinued by revelation to the President of the Church, Wilford Woodruff, in 1890. Though rarely preached and never practiced in Europe, it soon became the symbolic curse of Mormonism around the world,

a condition that lasted well into the twentieth century.

The doctrine and practice of polygamy created serious tensions in the Nauvoo Mormon community both before and after Joseph Smith's death. For some Mormons it was a difficult doctrine to believe and accept. Emma Smith, Joseph's wife, rejected it; Brigham Young, later the quintessential polygamist and target of countless cartoons, lampoons, and moral diatribes from around the world, himself originally found it difficult to accept.

Some of these my brethren know what my feelings were at the time Joseph revealed the doctrine; I was not desirous of shrinking from any duty, nor of failing in the least to do as I was commanded, but it was the first time in my life that I had desired the grave, and I could hardly get over it for a long time. And when I saw a funeral, I felt to envy the corpse

(continued on page 105)

The city of Nauvoo can be seen in the distance across the Mississippi River in 1907. Photo was taken from Montrose, Iowa. (Photo by George Edward Anderson)

visual images of Joseph Smith are among many handed down
ugh various sources and institutions. On page 100 is an alleged
otograph" copyrighted in the Library of Congress by Joseph
h III, the Prophet's son. On this page at lower right is an alleged
otograph" retouched by Salt Lake City artist Dan Weggeland
an alleged original daguerreotype. At the top left of this page
copy of a painting believed executed by William Major from
ame daguerreotype in 1844. At the top right of this page is an
ed "photograph" copyrighted in 1921 by Harrison Sperry of
Lake City. The notarized, sworn statement attached to the pho-
ph is shown below.

STATE OF UTAH, } ss.
COUNTY OF SALT LAKE. }

THIS PICTURE COPYRIGHTED IN
THE UNITED STATES

HARRISON SPERRY, first being duly sworn, deposes and says:

That William Crawford Anderson has this 17th day of October,
1921, shown to me a photograph of the Prophet Joseph Smith,
said by Mr. Anderson to have been obtained by him about two
years ago near Kirtland, Ohio, which photograph is a true picture
of the Prophet Joseph Smith.

That he was eleven years of age when he last saw the Prophet
and his memory of the Prophet's features and looks are clear and
vivid and distinct at this time.

That he had seen him about every day, sometimes more than
once, for weeks and months during the latter part of the Prophet's
life, and therefore the face and person of the Prophet had become
familiar to him, and he now unhesitatingly says that this picture
is the only real true likeness of the Prophet Joseph Smith that he
has seen since he saw him in life.   *Harrison Sperry*

Subscribed and sworn to before me this 17th day of October,
A. D 1921.   *Robert A. Burns*
                    (SEAL)   Notary Public
Residing at Salt Lake City, Utah, My commission expires Sept.
25, 1925.

ASSASSINATIO

OSEPH SMITH.

Piercy's sketches also included the room in the old jail where Joseph, Hyrum, and two other Mormons were imprisoned. The caretaker in the drawing is pointing to the bullet holes in the wall. (From Piercy's *Route from Liverpool to Great Salt Lake Valley*)

The old well where Joseph Smith was shot to death was still standing when Piercy sketched this scene with his *camera lucida* in 1853. (From Piercy's *Route from Liverpool to Great Salt Lake Valley*)

its situation, and to regret that I was not in the coffin, knowing the toil and labor that my body would have to undergo; and I have had to examine myself, from that day to this, and watch my faith, and carefully meditate, lest I should be found desiring the grave more than I ought to do. (*Journal of Discourses* 2:266)

Overleaf, pages 102–103: The assassination of Joseph Smith is depicted in this old woodcut from T.B.H. Stenhouse's 1873 history of the Mormon Church. A mob attacked the jail on June 27, 1844, killing Joseph and his brother, Hyrum. (From *Rocky Mountain Saints* by T.B.H. Stenhouse, New York, 1873)

Left: The old stone Carthage Jail is pictured on a bleak, overcast day in 1907. "Visited the jail where the prophet and patriarch were killed," photographer George Edward Anderson wrote in his diary under the entry for May 3. "... Saw the hole in the door made by the bullet, the window from which the prophet jumped. The well has been filled in, and is marked by some flowers put out in a circle. Made a negative of the old jail in a snow storm." (Photo by George Edward Anderson)

A sketch of the old jail was al[so]
drawn in 1853 by English arti[st]
Frederick Hawkins Pierc[e.]
"Having seen the place a[nd]
made my sketches," he wro[te]
later, "I was glad to leave. T[wo]
lives unatoned for, and 'blo[od]
crying from the ground,' ma[de]
the spot hateful." (From Pier[-]
cy's *Route from Liverpool* [to]
Great Salt Lake Valley)

Below: An old woodcut in St[en-]
house's *Rocky Mountain Sai[nts]*
depicts "the end" for Jose[ph]
Smith as his assassins prop h[im]
up against the old well and [fire]
bullets into his body. (Fr[om]
Stenhouse's *Rocky Mount[ain]*
Saints, 1873)

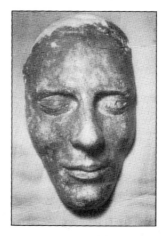

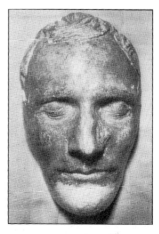

engraving of Hyrum Smith, Prophet's brother, may trace origins to an early daguer-otype made by Lucian Foster Nauvoo, Illinois, in 1843–44. (Brigham Young Uni-sity Archives)

An engraving of Joseph Smith's profile can probably trace its origins to the Sutcliffe Maud-sley caricature. (Brigham Young University Archives)

The death masks of Joseph and Hyrum Smith, made shortly after their murders in 1844, give an idea of the brothers' visual images, although their faces have undoubtedly been altered by the trauma they experienced in the multiple gunshot wounds received when a mob stormed the Carthage Jail in 1844. Joseph's face, on the left, closely matches the visual images in paintings and the alleged "photographs." Hyrum's face, on the right, also matches his visual images, but his death mask, in particular, has been distorted by a bullet that struck him in the face, just to the left of his nose. (Photos by Nelson Wadsworth, from the late Wilford Wood collection of Mormon memorabilia)

Left: Brigham Young, wearing tails and a stovepipe hat, poses a daguerreotypist in the early 1840s. This picture was possibly Lucian Foster in Nauvoo in 1843, more than a year before You assumed leadership of the Mormon Church. (Brigham Young U versity Photo Archives)

Opposite right, top: Mormon missionaries, in the foreground, v Water Street in Nauvoo on May 2, 1907. Photographer Geo Edward Anderson took this view from Hyrum Smith's barn, look toward Orson Pratt's and William Law's homes, as well as the cor lot where the old Mormon printing office stood. In the backgrou is the City of Nauvoo ferry boat. (Photo by George Edward , derson, May 2, 1907)

Overleaf, pages 108–109: A contemporary painting illustrates persecution and expulsion of the Mormons from Nauvoo in 18 The engraving says the print was "dedicated to Rev. Orson Hyd Hyde, an early church leader (see page 24, top right), was also ed of the *Frontier Guardian* in Iowa, 1849–1852. (Mormon Chu Historical Department)

Overleaf, pages 110–111: Ruins of the Nauvoo Temple were ne reduced to a pile of stones when Piercy sketched this view. incendiary had set fire to the building after the Mormons left Illi and headed for Utah. "The visitor's first steps are over evidence ruin and desolation," he wrote later, ". . . abandoned by their r less destroyers, and are now monuments of their selfish, jealous contemptible hate." (From Piercy's *Route from Liverpool to G Salt Lake Valley*)

Polygamy contributed significantly to the growth of anti-Mormon sentiment in western Illinois, where the populace soon formed violent mobs who found Mormonism reprehensible, feared its growing and united political power, and eventually took the law into its own hands. Joseph and Hyrum, his brother, were killed while in jail in June 1844 awaiting trial by those confident that the destruction of the charismatic prophet would destroy the church. This did not happen. Within a few months, the Mormons decided, as in Ohio and Missouri before, that they must leave, but not before new vigorous leadership under Brigham Young and the Apostles arose to keep most of the church intact and to make plans for the future. It was their quiet tribute to Joseph Smith as his era came to a close.

Opposite right, bottom: Mormons, driven from their homes few of life's necessities in the winter of 1846, camped here on Pot Slough near Montrose, Iowa, across the Mississippi River from N voo. It was here, said Brigham Young in his diary, "that the I sent flocks of quail, which lit upon their wagons and their er tables, and upon the ground within their reach . . ." Appare huge flocks of quail had attempted to cross the River on the 3 40 mile stretch occupied by the Mormons, on the same night had fled Nauvoo. But the flight was beyond the birds' strength, they dropped from the sky into the river boats and onto the b near the camps, providing food for the destitute pioneers and paring them for the hardships of the long "flight" that lay ahea they "pursued the phantom of a new home" in America's wes wilderness. (Photo by George Edward Anderson, May 2, 1907

When he passed Independence Rock in 1853, English artist Frederick Hawkins Piercy sketched the well-known geographic feature on the Mormon Trail. (*Route from Liverpool to Great Salt Lake Valley*, by Frederick Hawkins Piercy)

Mormon wagons gather in a circle at Independence Rock in this painting by William Henry Jackson. The huge, rounded earth formation was a favorite camping place for passing immigrants. Many inscribed their names on the rock before they proceeded on their journeys. (John F. Bennett Collection, Utah Historical Society)

Mary Ann Stucki Hafen, a Swiss girl of six, left this account of their family's trek in 1860:

> The train landed us at the point of outfit. Father was a carpenter, and they asked him to stop for a while and help make handcarts, as most of the people were too poor to buy teams.
>
> When we came to load up our belongings we found that we had more than we could take. Mother was forced to leave behind her feather bed, the bolt of linen, two large trunks full of clothes, and some other valuable things which we needed so badly later. Father could take only his most necessary tools. . . .
>
> There were six to our cart. Father and mother pulled it; Rosie (two years old) and Christian (six months old) rode; John (nine) and I (six) walked. Sometimes, when it was down hill, they let me ride too.

Father had bought a cow to take along, so we could have milk on the way. At first he tied her to the back of the cart, but she would sometimes hang back, so he thought he would make a harness and have her pull the cart while he led her. By this time mother's feet were so swollen that she could not wear shoes, but had to wrap her feet with cloth. Father thought that by having the cow pull the cart mother might ride. This worked well for some time.

One day a group of Indians came riding up on horses. Their jingling trinkets, dragging poles and strange appearance frightened the cow and set her chasing off with the cart and the children. We were afraid that the children might be killed, but the cow fell into a deep gully and the cart turned upside down. Although the children were under the trunk and bedding, they were unhurt, but after

Mormon immigrants pose in a group portrait for Salt Lake City photographer C.R. Savage in 1866. The photographer had made a 9,000-mile, circuitous trip by way of San Francisco, Panama, and New York to outfit a traveling darkroom and accompany a Mormon wagon train back to Salt Lake City. The original negatives of the trek were destroyed in a fire in his gallery in 1883. (Utah Historical Society)

family and earthly possessions they could take, most walked.

William Clayton, himself an English convert, captured the mood and spirit of the pioneers in what has become a classic Mormon hymn, "Come, Come Ye Saints":

Come, come, ye saints,
No toil nor labor fear,
But with joy wend your way.
Though hard to you this journey may appear,
Grace shall be as your day.
'Tis better far for us to strive,
Our useless cares from us to drive.
Do this and joy your heart will swell,
All is well, all is well.

And should we die,
Before our journey's through,
Happy day! All is well.
We then are free
From toil and sorrow, too.
With the just we shall dwell.
But if our lives are spared again,
To see the saints there rest obtain
Oh, How we'll make this chorus swell,
All is well, all is well.

To a later gifted writer, Wallace Stegner, the Mormon pioneers were

the most systematic, organized, disciplined, and successful pioneers in our history; and their advantage over the random individualists who preceded them and paralleled them and followed them up the valley of the Platte come directly from their "un-American" social and religious organization. . . . When their villages on wheels reached the valley of their destination, the Saints were able to revert at once, because they were town and temple builders and because they led their families with them, to the stable agrarian life in which most of them had grown up. (Stegner, 6)

Not a few of these immigrants were Europeans—no longer just Britons, but Danes, Swedes, Swiss, Germans, Norwegians, and a few from Italy and France; all had accepted the Mormon message preached by a growing number of missionaries who braved the elements, persecution, and police to spread a message they themselves had so recently embraced. Most immigrants saved what they could from meager incomes—only about one in twenty could afford to go—first to cross the sea, then to cross the plains to reach the new Zion in the West in the land of "unlimited opportunities."

For Europe's very poor, the idea of the handcarts was developed so that many more could come.

THE WESTWARD MOVEMENT

The westward trek of the Mormon pioneers, which began from Nauvoo in the winter of 1846 and ended in the Salt Lake Valley in 1847, is one of the best known parts of Mormon history. Before spring came, the first group of destitute Mormons heading west began to drive wagons across the frozen Mississippi into Iowa, or to ferry them through ice-filled waters. The rest of 1846 and early 1847 was spent in crossing the Iowa Territory, leaving a series of settlements and gardens along the way to house and nourish those who followed, and in building a Winter Quarters, a settlement on the Missouri River in the present city of Omaha, Nebraska. From there with the warming weather they could begin the thousand-mile trip west to the Great Basin in the Rocky Mountains, their new home.

Life was difficult on the trail and in the temporary settlements on both sides of the Missouri.

There were, as historian Stanley Kimball has emphasized, tragedies along the way—over the years perhaps as many as 6,000 died—but the trek was not so bad as many later Mormons have imagined. Exhaustion, exposure, disease, and lack of food stalked the Saints going west. Still, ". . . to the vast majority, . . . the experience was positive—a difficult and rewarding struggle." (Kimball, 153) Ten years after the first company that he was in "pioneered" the way, Heber C. Kimball recalled that the trek was ". . . pretty hard and laborious, I admit, but it was one of the pleasantest journeys I ever performed." (*Journal of Discourses* 5:132)

By 1869, in the two decades before the transcontinental railroad was completed, some 60,000 Mormons "crossed the plains"; some came on horseback, some drove or rode in covered wagons, some pushed inexpensive handcarts with whatever

Opposite left: A clump of cottonwood trees just opposite Winter Quarters marks the Council Bluffs Ferry, also known as "Ferryville," where Mormon wagons crossed the Missouri River and headed into Indian territory. (*Route from Liverpool to Great Salt Lake Valley*, by Frederick Hawkins Piercy)

Below: The Mormon exodus from Nauvoo is depicted in an old engraving from T.B.H. Stenhouse's book, *The Rocky Mountain Saints*. The Latter-day Saints fled Nauvoo in the middle of the winter of 1846 as mobs clamored at the gates of their city. (From *The Rocky Mountain Saints*, by T.B.H. Stenhouse)

that father did not hitch the cow to the cart again. He let three Danish boys take her to hitch to their cart. Then the Danish boys, each in turn, would help father pull our cart.

After about three weeks my mother's feet became better so she could wear her shoes again. She would get so discouraged and down-hearted; but father never lost courage. He would always cheer her up by telling her that we were going to Zion, that the Lord would take care of us, and that better times were coming.

Even when it rained the company did not stop traveling. A cover on the handcart shielded the two younger children. The rest of us found it more comfortable moving than standing still in the drizzle. In fording streams the men often carried the children and weaker women across on their backs. The company stopped over on Sundays for rest, and meetings were held for spiritual comfort and guidance. At night, when the handcarts were drawn up in a circle and the fires were lighted, the camp looked quite happy.

Singing, music, and speeches by the leaders cheered everyone. I remember that we stopped one night at an old Indian camp ground. There were many bright-colored beads in the ant hills.

At times we met or were passed by the overland stage coach with its passengers and mail bags and drawn by four fine horses. When the Pony Express dashed past it seemed almost like the wind racing over the prairie.

Our provisions began to get low. One day a herd of buffalo ran past and the men of our company shot two of them. Such a feast as we had when they were dressed. Each family was given a piece of meat to take along. My brother John, who pushed at the back of our cart, used to tell how hungry he was all the time and how tired he got from pushing. He said he felt that if he could just sit down for a few minutes he would feel so much better. But instead, father would ask if he couldn't push a little harder. Mother was nursing the baby and could not help much, especially when the food ran short

and she grew weak. When rations were reduced father gave mother a part of his share of the food, so he was not so strong either.

When we got that chunk of buffalo meat father put it in the handcart. My brother John remembered that it was the fore part of the week and that father said we would save it for Sunday dinner. John said, "I was so very hungry and the meat smelled so good to me while pushing the handcart that I could not resist. I had a little pocket knife and with it I cut off a piece or two each half day. Although I expected a severe whipping when father found it out, I cut off little pieces each day. I would chew them so long that they

got white and perfectly tasteless. When father came to get the meat he asked me if I had been cutting off some of it. I said 'Yes. I was so hungry I could not let it alone.' Instead of giving me a scolding or whipping, father turned away and wiped tears from his eyes."

Members of the Mormon Battalion halt on their long march to quench their thirsts and fill their canteens in this painting by George Martin Ottinger. The U.S. Army unit was recruited from the Mormon ranks as the immigrants began their journey across the plains. It distinguished itself in the war with Mexico by making one of the longest known marches in military history, covering a distance of more than 1,000 miles. (LDS Church Historical Department)

At last, when we reached the top of Emigration Canyon, overlooking Salt Lake, the whole company stopped to look down through the Valley. Some yelled and tossed their hats in the air. A shout of joy arose at the thought that our long trip was over, that we had at last reached Zion, the place of rest. We all gave thanks to God for helping us safely over the Plains and mountains to our destination.

When we arrived in the city we were welcomed by the people who came out carrying baskets of fruit and other kinds of good things to eat. Even though we could not understand their language, they made us feel that we were among friends.

Right: Wagons hold up for a "noon resting" near Coalville, Utah, in 1866 on the last leg of their trek across the plains to Salt Lake City. Photo was taken by C.R. Savage, a photographer who accompanied the wagon train on its journey to Salt Lake City. (John F. Bennett Collection, Utah Historical Society)

Below: Many children were included in the pioneer migrations. In this view, youngsters in the Burdick family pose in front of their wagons with their pet dog during a trip to Sunnyside, Utah, at the turn of the century. The migration to Carbon County was triggered by the discovery of rich coal deposits in central Utah and the opening of mines. (Photo by George Edward Anderson)

A Mormon wagon train crosses the Platte River on its way over the Mormon Trail, probably sometime in the 1860s. The photographer is unknown. (LDS Church Historical Department)

We were invited home by a good family who kept us two or three days, until my parents were rested. Then we were given a little house near the river Jordan, three miles from town, and father was put to work on the public road. He was paid in produce, mostly flour and potatoes, from the Tithing Office. (Hafen and Hafen 1:187–190)

European Mormon detractors often castigated these new Saints gathering in Liverpool from all over Europe as an unwashed rabble; respectable Christian civilization was well to be rid of them. But the English novelist Charles Dickens had a different view. In 1863 he boarded the "Amazon," loaded with Mormon emigrants, to see for himself. His sketch was later published in the "Uncommercial Traveller":

Now, I have seen emigrant ships before this day in June. And these people are so strikingly different from all other people in like circumstances whom I have ever seen, that I wonder aloud, "What *would* (italics in original) a stranger suppose these emigrants to be!" . . .

" 'A stranger would be puzzled to guess the right name for these people, Mr. Uncommercial,' says the captain."

"Indeed he would!"

"If you hadn't known, could you ever have supposed?"

"How could I! I should have said they were in their degree, the pick and flower of England!"

" 'So should I,' says the captain."

"How many are they?"

"Eight hundred in round numbers." (Mulder and Mortensen, 336–337)

Mormon emigrants were not typical. They did look for free land and the possibility of a higher standard of living promised them by church leaders, and also for freedom from traditions—economic, political, social, and religious—that, they believed had held them bound. But, as Conway Sonne has written,

> [They] were not driven by a dream of El Dorado or political paradise. Religion brought them to America and most of these converts expected little else but struggle and sacrifice in the wild country of their "gathering." Inevitably some faltered, defected and turned to more worldly interests. Yet the majority carried on and contributed substantially to the settlement of the American West. (Sonne, 137)

A Mormon wagon train emerges from Emigration Canyon and crosses the flats into Salt Lake Valley in a reenactment of the 1847 trek during the 50th Jubilee Celebration in 1897. (John F. Bennett Collection, Utah Historical Society)

Most, like Jacob Tobler, truly came "for the Gospel's sake," leaving behind and never to see again family, friends, and homeland for a life of "society with the Saints." His story is typical for most of the Mormon immigrants.

Born and reared in the rural beauty of the eastern Swiss canton of Appenzell, he and his new bride, Katherine, became Mormons in August 1857 when a newly converted zealous Mormon missionary from Zürich ventured into the eastern valleys in search of souls. They soon joined the small but growing congregation in Herisau where they learned more about Mormonism and helped bring in another dozen converts, while at the same time saving what money they could spare from his weaver's salary. Together with some help from the church's own Perpetual Emigration Fund, they prepared to emigrate to Utah. By 1861 they joined a larger group leaving Switzerland that spring, taking what was becoming the familiar route down the Rhine and across the North Sea to Liverpool. Here they became two of the 950 European Mormons—Brit-

ons, Scandinavians, Swiss, and Germans—who sailed on the "Monarch of the Sea" to New York. Earlier Mormon immigrants had come via New Orleans, Philadelphia, or Boston, but after 1850 most followed this same path.

The railroad took them as far as Winter Quarters where, like other Mormon immigrants before and after, Katherine died of cholera. Jacob came on alone as a member of Sextus Johnston's company in pursuit of their common dream; he walked most of the thousand miles, arriving September 28, 1861 to the usual friendly welcome in Salt Lake City.

By that fall of 1861 the Mormons had been in the Great Basin for fourteen years; according to the census of 1860, Salt Lake City was a respectable community of 8,200 people, and growing so rapidly that by 1870 it would be half again as large. Fifty-eight other settlements had been established in Utah with numerous others in surrounding states and as far away as San Bernardino, California. Brigham Young had already gained a reputation both in the United States and abroad as the "American Moses" who had led his people west and had founded a marvelous empire. To Moritz Busch, Young was an Asiatic despot with "energy, understanding of human nature and administrative talent, but no 'genius'." But he was much more. He was also a great colonizer and for Mormons like Jacob Tobler and his descendants, a prophet of God. Indeed, one of the motivations for Jacob as well as for thousands of other European Mormons to join the church in the first place and then "gather to Zion" was to be able to live their lives and rear their children in the society of "Apostles and Prophets."

Jacob Tobler left no record of his impressions of Salt Lake City or of Utah, but a contemporary, British adventurer-writer Sir Richard Burton, gave a rather full account of his month-long stay there the year before. The first view of the Salt Lake Valley overwhelmed the well-traveled visitor so that "... even I could not ... gaze upon the scene without emotion." Burton had also been alerted to look for the signs of polygamy but was disappointed.

> I ... looked in vain for the outhouse harems, in which certain romancers concerning things Mormon had informed me that wives are kept like any other stock. I presently found this but one of a multitude of delusions. Upon the whole, the Mormon settlement was a vast improvement upon its contemporaries in the valleys of the Mississippi and the Missouri. (Mulder and Mortensen, 331)

Like many a Mormon immigrant in the nineteenth century, Jacob Tobler did not remain in Salt Lake City, but was "called" by church leaders to join another dozen Swiss families and help settle the community of Santa Clara, some 350 miles to the south and west. From their lush homeland they

This pioneer odometer was invented by two men who made the initial trek to Utah in 1847 and was used by Brigham Young on one wagon to measure the distance from the Missouri River to the Great Salt Lake Valley. The difference between the measurements of this crude instrument and those made by government surveyors who later passed over the same route with more sophisticated instruments was only 60 feet. (Temple Square Museum)

THE PIONEER ODOMETER.

This machine was invented by two of the Pioneers who crossed the Great Plains in 1847, and was used by Brigham Young and his company to measure the distance from the Missouri River to Salt Lake Valley. The difference between the measurements made with this instrument and those made by the government surveyors, who subsequently passed over the route, was less than 60 feet.

had been called into a scorching desert. Brigham Young was striving to make his Kingdom not only partially autonomous within the United States, but also self-supporting in its economy. That meant Mormons were to grow and manufacture what they needed and not buy from non-Mormons or import from the eastern United States.

Santa Clara was in Utah's "Dixie," where the much milder climate permitted the cultivation of cotton, grapes, melons, and vegetables. Though little of permanent value would come of the cotton-raising scheme, Jacob earned his living and supported his growing family largely from the productivity of a small farm. In this he was like most Mormons of the nineteenth century, living in scattered small rural communities in the Mormon Kingdom which stretched from Southern Idaho into Arizona.

Before he could leave Salt Lake City, however, this twenty-eight-year-old widower needed to find another wife. He remembered a young Swiss woman, Barbara Staheli from Thurgau, who had been part of their overland company; she agreed, and they were married and joined the Swiss company headed south. Subsequently, Jacob became part of the estimated 10 to 15 percent of the Mormons who

practiced polygamy, having two wives at one time. While they knew of polygamous families with discord and unhappiness, their arrangement worked out well. From the three Utah wives (Katherine had no children) came twenty-one children and, to date, hundreds of descendants. Children of the fourth wife, Rosena Reber Staheli Tobler, remembered that after their mother died they were reared by "Aunt Barbara", who was more "partial" to them than to her own children.[18] Jacob and family became integral parts of the community where they found warmth, friendship, and security.

Life was focused on the church ward or parish; Jacob and several members of his family helped provide the leadership of the ward and community for the next sixty years. Economically, the large family was able to survive, if not prosper, by raising and selling produce, but also by Jacob's keeping books for the church, the school, and the community irrigation company. They were even financially able, as most Mormon families desired, to send one son, William, back to Switzerland and Germany as a missionary at the turn of the century. There, William met his father's family, but while they received him warmly they wanted nothing to do with his religion. He also experienced the standard treatment for missionaries by spending time in prison in Dresden.

Above and opposite left: A map produced during the Pioneer Jubilee Celebration in 1897 shows the day-by-day progress of the Mormons in 1847 as their wagons crossed Wyoming. The portion of the map at left shows the pioneer wagons' movement from the Sweetwater River, past Fort Bridger, into Utah and finally into the Great Salt Lake Valley. (Utah Historical Society)

The adobe-walled Fort Laramie on the North Platte River in Wyoming is sketched by Frederick Hawkins Piercy in 1853. The fort consisted of a military post and post office and was about midway between Winter Quarters and the Great Salt Lake Valley. (*Route from Liverpool to Great Salt Lake Valley*, by Frederick Hawkins Piercy)

A souvenir post card for Covered Wagon Days in 1931 features photos of Brigham Young, covered wagons, and a buffalo skull marker left by the pioneers on the plains in 1847. Written on the skull is this message: "Pioneers camped here June 3rd, 1847. Making 15 miles today. All well. Brigham Young." The skull was found at a pioneer encampment near Independence Rock. (John F. Bennett Collection, Utah Historical Society)

Like most Mormons, the larger Tobler family received the rudiments of an elementary education but not much more; it was not until the next generation that Jacob's grandchildren began to go to college. Cultural opportunities in such communities were also limited, but having learned to play the drum while a soldier in Switzerland Jacob enjoyed playing in a band organized by his fellow countryman, George Staheli.

Left: An old photograph taken before 1869 shows the mail station and settlement on the Weber River at the mouth of Echo Canyon, a favorite stopping off place for wagon trains and later for construction of the railroad. (Utah State University Special Collections)

ht: A settlement grew up
und Fort Bridger, a favorite
pping place for pioneers.
ws of log houses line streets
the old fort in 1865, when
photograph was taken.
ah State University Special
lections)

posite left: Mountain Man
Bridger met the Mormon
neers in 1847 on their way
Utah and wagered Brigham
ing that they would be un-
e to grow crops in the al-
ne soils of the Salt Lake
ey. Bridger was the first
wn white man to look upon
Great Salt Lake. (C. W.
er Collection, LDS Church
corical Department)

ioneer family with their ox and mule team arrive in Salt Lake City, pausing in front of one of the pioneer-built walls of the Old Fort.
n F. Bennett Collection, Utah Historical Society)

Above: The Mormon settlement of Great Salt Lake City begin[s] rise from the valley floor in 1853 when it is sketched by Frede[rick] Hawkins Piercy. The English artist used a *camera lucida* to d[raw] accurately this pioneer scene, even down to the shadows of the cl[oud] hanging over the city in the foreground. (*Route from Liverpo[ol to] Great Salt Lake Valley*, by Frederick Hawkins Piercy)

Left: Another technically accurate view of Great Salt Lake Cit[y in] 1851 is contained in this pencil sketch, said to be copied from [an] original daguerreotype taken by Californian J. Wesley Jones. [The] daguerreotypist made some 1,500 views of western America [on a] trip from the Missouri River to San Francisco in 1851, but [the] originals have been lost, and only some pencil sketches copied f[rom] the daguerreotypes remain, including this one of Great Salt L[ake] City. (California Historical Society)

Left: An old lithograph shows what the Mormon settlement of G[reat] Salt Lake City looked like in 1850. Engraved in the right-hand co[rner] in small letters is "Ackerman Lith. 379 Broadway, N.Y." (Joh[n C.] Bennett Collection, Utah Historical Society)

A yoke of oxen pull a small covered wagon in pioneer Utah, probably sometime in the 1860s. (Utah State University Special Collections)

Hollywood's version of the Mormon settlement of Great Salt Lake City is shown in this photograph of the set for the 1940s motion picture *Brigham Young*. Producer Cecil B. DeMille researched the early history of the city to build this technically accurate setting for his film. Utah's Wasatch Mountains are in the background. (Brigham Young University Photo Archives)

BRIGHAM YOUNG AND THE GREAT BASIN KINGDOM: 1847–1896

The Great Basin Kingdom that Brigham Young founded in 1847 was, in his mind, truly a kind of theocratic Kingdom within the loose framework of the United States. Mormons were and remained staunch supporters of the United States and its constitution, but on numerous occasions had been disappointed by those with political power. In Ohio, Missouri, and Nauvoo, they had not only done without the desired and deserved protection from the anarchic mobs, but also were persecuted by the governments themselves. When Joseph Smith's appeals for federal protection to the President of the United States, Martin Van Buren, fell on deaf ears, he became frightfully aware of the Mormon lack of political security. He eventually launched his own serious but unsuccessful candidacy for the presidency in 1844. The trek into the West was largely an attempt to get away to a place no one else wanted, where "none would hurt or make afraid" as William Clayton poetically wrote.

But in many ways the Mormon conflict with American political authority was just beginning. In 1857, ten years after the original settlers arrived, President James Buchanan, acting on bad advice from "unsavory" federal appointees in Utah, dispatched the U.S. Army to put down the Mormon "rebellion." The "Utah War," as it was called, turned out to be no war at all, but rather "Buchanan's blunder." The army had been dispatched across the country at considerable expense; Mormon guerrilla activity and the onset of winter slowed progress, destroyed supplies, and forced them to winter in burned-out Fort Bridger. Following the mediation of a friend, Col. Thomas L. Kane, the army arrived in Salt Lake City in June 1858 to find it quiet and deserted. There was no war. It was as James Allen and Glen Leonard have written, "an army of occupation that never needed to be sent." (Allen and Leonard, 309) Still, it left open wounds of mutual distrust that would take generations to heal. It also stirred up passions that led to the Mountain Meadows Massacre, a crime committed by Mormons and Indians against a party of California-bound immigrants from Arkansas and Missouri and that tarnished the Mormon reputation

(continued on page 147)

A cluster of tepees marks a temporary settlement of the nomadic Ute Indian Tribe in eastern Utah's Uintah Basin sometime in the 1870s. (Photo by William Henry Jackson, Utah Historical Society)

Opposite left: Brigham Young is photographed in 1858 in the Lion House in Salt Lake City, shortly after Johnston's Army invaded Utah. Although the United States had sent troops to put down the so-called Mormon rebellion, the expedition was deemed a failure and became known as "President Buchanan's blunder." (LDS Church Historical Department)

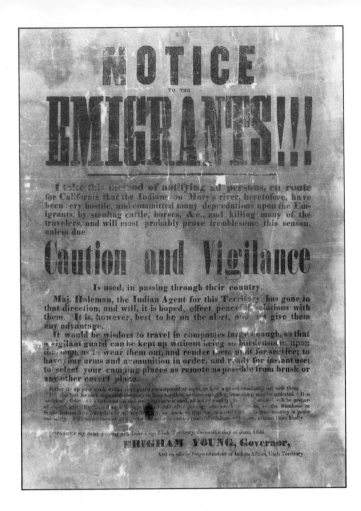

Left: A handbill circulated by Brigham Young in the summer o[f] 1852 warns emigrants about the dangers of Indian depredation[s]. (LDS Church Historical Department)

Opposite right: An Indian from the Shoshone Tribe shows off h[is] native dress in C.R. Savage's Gallery in Salt Lake City in the 1870[s]. (Photo by C.R. Savage, LDS Church Historical Department)

Below: Members of the Ute Indian Tribe gather for a powwow [in] the Uintah Basin sometime in the 1860s or 1870s. Congress esta[b]lished the Uintah Valley Indian Reservation by treaty in 1864, b[ut] war between the Mormons and the Utes broke out when pressur[e] was exerted to remove the Utes to that desolate location. The Bla[ck] Hawk War, named after the Ute chief at the time, lasted for mo[re] than three years and substantially delayed the Mormon settleme[nt] of the outlying areas. (Photo by Charles W. Carter, LDS Chur[ch] Historical Department)

Another Utah Indian friendly to the Mormons was Chief Kanosh, shown here sometime around 1872, when he was named to a special delegation to Washington, D.C., to mediate peace in Utah's Black-Hawk Indian War. (LDS Church Historical Department)

Below: Members of the Shivwits Indian tribe in southwestern Utah were baptized in a shallow stream near Santa Clara in 1875. The white man in the water is Daniel D. McArthur, then president of the Mormon Stake (ecclesiastical district) in St. George. Standing on the rock is Washington County Sheriff Augustus P. Hardy, one of the first Mormon settlers in Santa Clara. (From John F. Bennett Collection, Utah Historical Society)

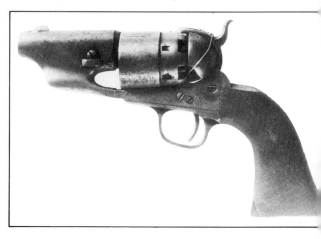

Left: Orrin Porter Rockwell, the so-called Mormon-destroying ang[el] sported long locks of hair and a beard when this photo was tak[en] in the 1870s in the twilight of his life. Rockwell was a color[ful] frontiersman always in the forefront of battling the Mormon cau[se] even if it meant use of firearms. (Utah Historical Society)

Below: Rockwell carried a sawed-off Colt, which could be loa[ded] with buckshot and be as effective as a miniature shotgun. The pis[tol] is now in the Mormon Church's gun collection and is kept loc[ked] in a vault. (Utah Historical Society)

Col. Lot Smith was one of the heros in the Utah War. With a command of only a handful of men, he burned Colonel Johnston's supply wagons, thus delaying the approach of Johnston's Army in Salt Lake City. Smith's military mission was one of the first examples of hit-and-run guerrilla fighting in modern warfare. (Utah State University Library Special Collections)

hn Doyle Lee, a Mormon ecclesiastical leader in Southern Utah, as accused of perpetrating the 1857 Mountain Meadows Massacre, which a wagon train of Missouri emigrants passing through Utah s slaughtered by Indians. (Utah State University Library Special ollections)

n Doyle Lee, the man sitting, waits on the edge of his coffin for ring squad to execute him for his role in the Mountain Meadows ssacre. Lee was excommunicated from the Mormon Church in 0, and a firing squad executed him for the crime seven years r. (Utah State University Library Special Collections)

146

in the United States and Europe for decades to come. Years later, John D. Lee, a leading Mormon in the area, was hanged for his part in the affair. (Arrington and Bitton, 169–170)

A growing non-Mormon population in Utah and reform-minded politicians and public opinion in the rest of the country turned their attention, once slavery had been abolished through the Civil War, to the other "relic of barbarism," polygamy, and the monolith of Mormon political authority in Utah. The first federal legislation against polygamy was passed in 1862 but, preoccupied with the Civil War, President Lincoln chose not to enforce it. "You tell Brigham Young if he will leave me alone, I'll leave him alone" (quoted by Arrington and Bitton, 170), Lincoln told a church representative, T.B.H. Stenhouse.

But such a *modus vivendi* would not persist. One attempt after another to gain statehood foundered on the Scylla of Mormon political dominance and the Charybdis of polygamy. Congress passed bill after bill culminating in the Edmunds-Tucker Act of 1887, which drew the political noose around the Mormons ever tighter. Prominent polygamous Mormons such as George Reynolds and George Q. Cannon contested the laws and were sent to prison, both originally because they believed the laws violated the freedom of religion clause in the Constitution and, more important, because polygamy was to them God's higher law to which they were bound. The attitude of loyal church members toward the wave of anti-polygamy legislation was captured earlier in 1882 by the consummate diarist and later Church President, Wilford Woodruff:

> It is entirely a breach of the Constitution of the United States; condemns men before trial or conviction by court or jury;

Opposite left: "The Carrion Crow in the Eagle's Nest" was how cartoonist Victor Gillam of *Puck* portrayed Mormonism in 1882, during the peak of sensational yellow journalism period in American media history. (From *Puck* [original in color], Jan. 22, 1882)

Below: *Harper's Weekly* published this highly sensational drawing depicting the alleged "frightful scene of carnage and desolation at the sack of Salt Lake City by United States troops." But the drawing was pure fiction because when it ran Johnston's Army had not yet even marched on Salt Lake City, and a special commission was in the process of negotiating a permanent peace. (*Harper's Weekly*, May 22, 1858)

FRIGHTFUL SCENE OF CARNAGE AND DESOLATION AT THE SACK OF SALT LAKE CITY BY THE UNITED STATES TROOPS. (*By our own Special Electric Designer.*)

Above: A montage of photographs shows Brigham Young with 19 of his wives. The Mormon prophet's practice of polygamy was often the target of attacks from anti-Mormons. (Utah Historical Society)

Opposite right: The stereotype of a Mormon elder favoring a young new wife is depicted in this political cartoon published in *Frank Leslie's Illustrated Newspaper* in 1886. The elder in the cartoon looks curiously like Brigham Young. (*Frank Leslie's Illustrated Newspaper*, May 8, 1886)

Left: Brigham Young and wife Margaret Pierce pose in this 1850s portrait. The photo is rare because the Mormon prophet was reluctant to be photographed with his wives. (Copied from original daguerreotype in possession of Mrs. Lorenzo S. Young)

takes away the right of trial by jury of their peers; makes an *ex post facto* law and a bill a attainder; takes away from the Latter-day Saints, because of their religious convictions, the franchise, and deprives them from sitting on juries because of their opinions but, if the nation can stand it, we can. It is taking a stand against Christ and His Kingdom, and against His people. (Cowley, 539)

Some polygamous church leaders, including Church President John Taylor, were forced into hiding from marshals intent on their arrest. The Edmunds-Tucker Act disincorporated the church; confiscated all church property worth more than $50,000; required voters, jurors, and office holders to take a test oath; forced lawful wives to testify against their husbands; and enforced numerous other restrictions. The power of the U.S. Government was arrayed against the church.

In September 1890 Woodruff, then President of the Church, proclaimed what has since been known as the "Manifesto," an official declaration stating that the church had already halted the

Above: Brigham Young strikes a rakish pose in C.R. Savage's photo gallery in 1871, at a time when the Mormon practice of polygamy was under intense fire from the federal government. (From an album in the Beehive House, Salt Lake City)

Mormon Apostle George Q. Cannon, seated center holding bouquet, is photographed with other Mormon leaders in Sugar House Territorial Prison in 1885. A number of prominent Mormons were incarcerated for practicing polygamy. (Utah Historical Society)

teaching of plural marriage and would not allow anyone to enter into the practice. A few weeks later the Manifesto was approved by the church membership. An era was coming to an end.

Six years later Utah was admitted as the forty-fifth state in the Union and the church began a policy of accommodation with established governments that has lasted throughout the twentieth century. A combination of accepting political realities along with revelation had led the Mormons, long known for their ability to endure and even thrive under persecution, to take this step. For some Mormons that acceptance was difficult, as some plural marriages were still contracted after 1890. But there can be little doubt that in the long run it was right and of great benefit to the church. It was also a good example of the church's ability to balance continuity and change. In spite of what some Mormons had said, polygamy was not basic to salvation; it could be put aside in order for the church to continue to exist and carry out its larger destiny.

Polygamy probably served a useful purpose in raising up a numerous posterity deeply imbued with the values of their fathers. But it may also be true that the discontinuance of it as well as the abandonment of the idea of a temporal and political kingdom of God in preparation for Christ's millennial reign gradually allowed Mormons to focus more clearly on the primacy of their spiritual and transcendent message and to bring it more forcefully to the world. While polygamy was practiced it became a "badge of courage" for Mormons, accentuating a kind of "artificial" peculiarity, giving them a kind of superiority vis-à-vis a sinful world, and promoting a defensiveness that was antithetical to their larger objectives. When it was gone Mormons were forced to rediscover and practice their true uniqueness in a more acceptable world.

For non-Mormons polygamy had been a lightning rod, illuminating and identifying a "fanaticism" that first, to the traditional Christians and then to the secularized and sophisticated, meant that one did not need to inquire about what Mormons believed or take them or their religion seriously.

While earnest moral voices strove to end the moral "blight," cartoonists and humorists took full advantage of the opportunities polygamy afforded

(continued on page 154)

Ann Eliza Webb Young, who sued Brigham Young for divorce in 1873, is shown in this late 1870s portrait, after she wrote a best-selling book against Mormon polygamy and went on a national speaking tour. (Photo by Charles W. Carter, LDS Church Historical Department's Carter Collection)

...ham Young's carriage waits in the muddy street in Salt Lake City during the Mormon leader's divorce trial brought by the so-called ...ly wife, Ann Eliza Webb Young. Court is being held before Chief Justice James McKean upstairs, above the livery stable in 1875. (Copied ... original *cartes de visite* in Donald H. Pickett collection)

them. Richard Cracroft, a Mormon scholar, has shown how influential American humorists Artemus Ward and Mark Twain knowingly perpetuated a myth about Mormons that they knew from personal experience was not true. Ward had quipped that "in Utah all the pretty girls mostly marry Young" while Twain's belittling of polygamy is captured in an account of how "some porky old frog of an elder, or a bishop marries a girl—likes her, takes another—likes her, marries her mother—likes her, marries her father, grandfather, great grandfather, and comes back hungry and asks for more." (Quoted in Cracroft, 200, 208)

While the political and polygamy struggles were going on in the 1870s and 1880s, the church was also consolidating itself within. New organizations were established to teach the children and youth Gospel principles, and in this way help them to better cope with the changing world and times. Mormons were learning that a new generation growing up in the predominantly Mormon communities were not necessarily understanding fundamental Mormon teachings or gaining faith in Mormonism. Already in the 1860s George Q. Cannon, a native Englishman and counselor to three church presidents, was troubled with the meager understanding of Mormon doctrines by the youth of his day. He therefore began to organize Sunday schools and published the *Juvenile Instructor* to remedy the problem. (Jensen, 42) Moreover, more of the "outside" world with its allurements was intruding into Mormon society. The transcontinental railroad that made it easier for converts to gather also brought adventuresome Gentiles to the Mormon Kingdom. Hence, a new awareness of the need to teach the doctrines and help the next generation to have its own existential confrontation with the faith began to emerge.

Part of the responsibility fell to developing a church educational system. From its beginning the church had placed significant emphasis upon education. In revelations to Joseph Smith, Mormons were told that "the glory of God is intelligence, or in other words, light and truth" and later that

Covered wagons are parked in front of pioneer business establishments in frontier Salt Lake City in the late 1850s. Photo shows a downtown block on the west side of Main Street. (Copied from an original albumen print in a private collection)

. . . whatever principle of intelligence we attain unto in this life it will rise with us in the resurrection. And if a person gains more knowledge and intelligence in this life through his diligence and obedience than another, he will have so much the advantage in the world to come. (Doctrine & Covenants 93:36; 130:18, 19)

Joseph Smith carried out this commitment by conducting a School of the Prophets for the education of some of his associates before the Mormons went west. Afterward, they established schools, first elementary and then secondary, in their wards and communities, until a free public education system was set up after the turn of the century. The church's commitment to education in the twentieth century, both philosophically and financially, has marched step-for-step with its own growth.

German converts contributed significantly to the educational achievements in Utah. Most well known among Mormons is the career of Dr. Karl Gottfried Maeser, a gifted Saxon schoolmaster, while another German, younger than Maeser, Louis

Dr. Karl G. Maeser, a native of Meissen, Germany, introduced the German philosophy of education into the Mormon culture in the 1870s. He was the first principal of Brigham Young Academy in Provo, which would evolve into Brigham Young University, one of the largest private universities in the United States. (BYU Photo Archives)

Moench, was for thirty years the heart and soul of education in northern Utah. Having become disillusioned with traditional Christianity, Maeser happened to read one of the many pamphlets denouncing Mormonism then extant in Europe. He thought the accusations extreme and unreasonable and made contact with Mormon authorities to learn more first hand.

Missionaries came covertly to Dresden where Maeser was taught and through an unusual spiritual manifestation converted to the church in 1855. As a result, he was forced to abandon his teaching post and leave Saxony, eventually to find a new home in the American West. After serving missions for the church in England and Germany interspersed with nearly vain attempts to earn a living as a tutor, teacher, and part-time professor at the University of Utah, Maeser was appointed, in 1876 by Brigham Young, as principal of the one-year-old Brigham Young Academy in Provo, forty miles south of Salt Lake City.

Here he found fame and honor, though not fortune, in the hearts of hundreds of grateful students including many of Mormonism's most distinguished leaders in the twentieth century. His extraordinary skill and zeal in teaching his philosophy of education—a combination of Wilhelm von Humboldt's dignity and development of the individual personality, Pestalozzian pedagogy and Mormon theology—made him the dominant personality in Mormon education well beyond his death in 1901. (Maeser, passim; Tobler, 325–344) In subsequent years church education would have conflicts with the secularizing forces, especially evolution and higher criticism. Still, the Mormon system, eventually joined with the growing public educational systems around the world, has succeeded in the past decades in providing the ever-expanding generations of Mormon youth with the educational tools and training to raise them into the middle class and permit them to compete in an industrial and urban society. Today, Maeser's major achievement, Brigham Young University, has become one of the largest private universities in the United States and the academically respectable flagship of a system bringing religious instruction and higher education to more than 750,000 students worldwide.

The relative peace, permanence, and prosperity of late nineteenth century Mormon society permitted renewed attention to the building of new temples to replace those left in Kirtland and Nauvoo. Upon the arrival of the first pioneer company in 1847, Brigham Young had marked with his cane the spot where the temple would be built, but it was not begun until 1853. Not until forty years later was this neo-Gothic masterpiece completed and dedicated, and it soon became the visual symbol of Mormonism throughout the world.

For some Mormons, such as James E. Talmage, one of the best-educated and later a church apostle, the dedication of the Salt Lake Temple was the beginning of a new era. In his journal he noted Church President Woodruff's comments on the new unity of the church leadership, especially

(continued on page 163)

A crowd gathers sometime in the 1860s on East Temple Street in downtown Salt Lake City to witness a "one-legged man walking on a tightrope," or so reads the caption written on the negative by the photographer. (Photo by Charles W. Carter, from original negative, LDS Church Historical Department)

*Ensign Peak.

Old wall around
the City.
⊙ White.
Private residences
Peach Orchards &c.

✕ white =
Kimball's En-
closure.

Entrance to
Temple Block
Bowery,
Tabernacle, &c.

Wall around the
Temple enclosure.

⊚ Position of Principal water co
from City Creek, ri
across the pictur

<u>Heber C. Kimball's Res</u>

158

† white cross
Mouth of City
Creek Cañon.

* White Star
Indian tents by
the old city wall

* Entrance to,
Tithing Office
Warerooms
Prest. Young's
enclosure.

Clear running
water

Main, or East Temple Street, in front of you.
Brig. Young's residence off here.
on what is called 1st South Temple St.

& left
walls. Clear running water.

G. S. L. City, 1864.

159

Overleaf, pages 158–159: An early photograph of the frontier settlement of Salt Lake City has been carefully captioned by a pioneer in the borders. The wall in the left foreground surrounds Temple Square before the Temple was built, and the one across the street surrounds the Tithing Office. The photo, copied from an old albumen print with the captions carefully drawn in India ink, can be dated in the late 1850s. It was printed from one of the earliest known wet-plate negatives made in Utah. (Copied from an old albumen print in a private collection)

This page, top left: The General Tithing and Storehouse, also kno[wn] as the Deseret Store, stands on the corner of Main and South Tem[ple] Streets, the main intersection in downtown Salt Lake City. A la[nd]mark building, formerly the Hotel Utah, stands on this spot too[.] Photograph, circa 1860, shows the main storehouse for food [and] supplies tithed by members of the Mormon faith in pioneer U[tah.] (Photo by Marsena Cannon, LDS Church Historical Departme[nt]) This page, top right: Salt Lake City's Main Street about 1869 sho[ws] the beginnings of Zions Cooperative Mercantile Institution, incl[ud]ing the Globe Warehouse of Naisbitt and Hindley, purchasing age[nts] for the Mormon cooperative association's stores. (Utah Histor[ical] Society)

ove: *The Mormon Tribune* and Dinwoodey's Cabinet Shop are sed in this building in downtown Salt Lake City in the 1870s. e anti-Mormon newspaper first began publication in 1870 and n the *Salt Lake Herald* was the beginning of the present day *Salt e Tribune*. (Utah Historical Society)

Above: The old Council House, built on the southwest corner of Main and South Temple streets in 1850, was the first public building in Utah. East Temple Street, as Main Street was known then, was dubbed "Whiskey Street" in the 1860s after an influx of non-Mormons brought saloons to downtown Salt Lake City. (Utah Historical Society)

Below: Freight wagons pause on the trail on their way to Mormon settlements in the 1880s. Even after the completion of the transcontinental railroad in 1869, covered wagons were used to ship goods to Utah's outlying communities. (Photo by George Edward Anderson, BYU Photo Archives)

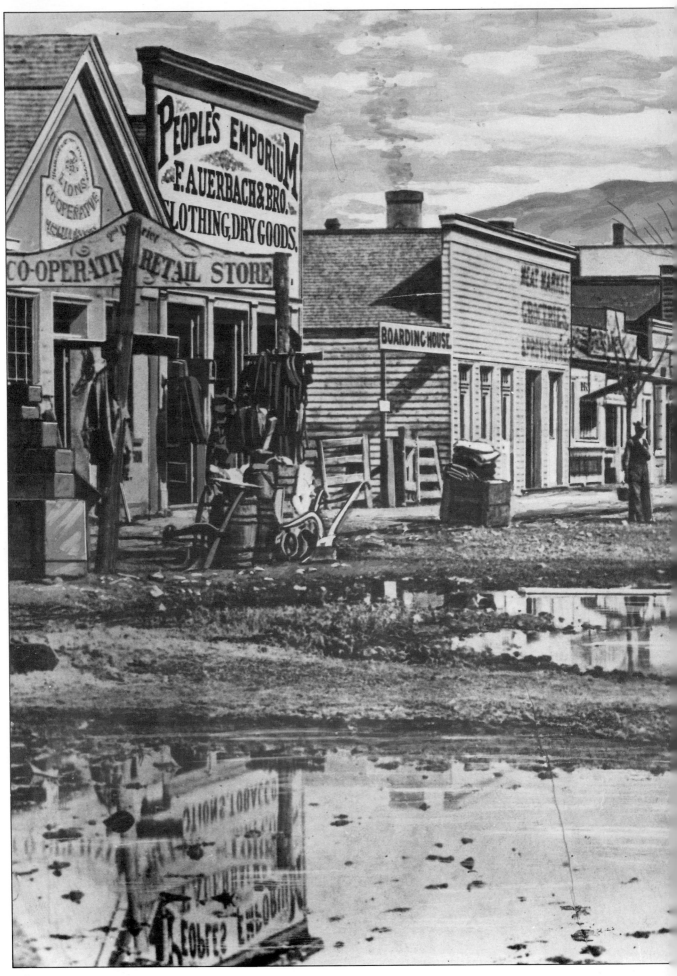

Mud puddles create obstacles in the dirt streets of downtown Ogden, Utah, in 1869. The Mormon cooperative ZCMI, left, exists side by side with the non-Mormon People's Emporium, owned by the Auerbach brothers. (From Herbert S. Auerbach collection at Lagoon Corp.)

on political matters, while his counselor, George Q. Cannon,

> referred to the remarkable and almost unprecedented change of public opinion toward this people during the last few months. . . . we can acknowledge this great revolution in feeling as a result of the Lord's goodness, and of His gracious promises, invoked perhaps, by the fastings, prayers and faith of the people. There were no strange or bewildering manifestations of "supernatural" agencies during the service, but the power of God was there, and the entire assembly felt it. (Talmage 7:5)

In the meantime, from 1877 on, three other stately temples in St. George, Logan, and Manti had been erected throughout the state.

ʇers in the Utah Woolen Mills pause from their labors at their looms to have their photograph taken, probably in the 1860s. (Photo by
ʇes W. Carter, LDS Church Historical Department Carter Collection)

ʙsite left: Amanda and Samuel Chambers were among the first
converts to the Mormon Church. Both embraced Mormonism
ʋes in the South, came west to Utah after the Civil War, and
ʇ in the southeast section of Salt Lake Valley, where they
ered. Chambers lived to the ripe old age of 98. At the time of
ʇath he was a man of wealth and owned a 30-acre estate. (LDS
ʇh Historical Department)

Overleaf, pages 166–167: An eagle with outstretched wings, sculpted
from five blocks of cedar by pioneer woodcarvers Ralph Ramsey and
William Bell, stands atop the Eagle Gate at the entrance to the estate
of Brigham Young. On the left is the Mormon prophet's residence,
called the Beehive House. (Photo by Charles W. Carter, from original
negative, LDS Church Historical Department)

Mormon missionaries on their way east pause at camp in Echo Canyon to have their picture taken. Despite persecutions from around world, the LDS Church continued to send out missionaries to proselytize and continued to gain converts from around the world. (Photo Charles W. Carter, LDS Church Historical Department Carter Collection)

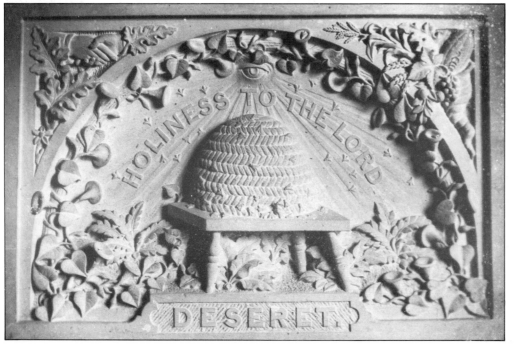

Opposite right: The most famous portrait of Brigham Young was taken by Charles R. Savage in 1876, less than a year before the prophet's death. (From an original albumen print on the wall of the Beehive House, Salt Lake City)

Left: A block of Utah oolitic limestone, sculptured with the name of the State of Deseret, was sent in 1853 as the state's contribution to the Washington Monument. This photograph was taken by Marsena Cannon in Salt Lake City before the stone was shipped. (Copied from an original daguerreotype, LDS Church Historical Department)

Mormon immigrants from Europe congregate at Castle Garden in New York in 1878 on their way to Utah. Drawing, made by a sketch ar
was published in *Frank Leslie's Illustrated Newspaper*. Thousands of converts made the perilous ocean voyage every year to join with th
Church in the tops of the Rocky Mountains. (From *Frank Leslie's Illustrated Newspaper*, Jan. 22, 1878)

QUOTATIONS
OF
FOREIGN COINS
& BANK NOTES

SALT LAKE

Above: Utah farm families work together to thresh grain sometime in the 1890s in central Utah. Photograph shows primitive, horse-powered farm machinery used before turn of the century. (Photo by Charles Ellis Johnson, BYU Photo Archives)

Homesteaders clear sagebrush on raw land in Emery County, Utah, sometime before the turn of the century. Agriculture and farming were the mainstays of the economy of Mormonism. (Photo by George Edward Anderson, BYU Photo Archives)

The flamboyant masthead of *The Mormon*, a bold, weekly newspaper published in New York City, attempt to illustrate the creed of Mormonism. The periodical was edited by John Taylor and defended the Morm point of view in the East between 1854 and 1856. (Utah Historical Society)

Left: Serge Louis Ballif (1821–1901) came from a prominent afflu family with strong pietistic traditions and converted to Mormon in 1852. He was later president of the Swiss-German Mission a father of large, faithful, and influential posterity.

Opposite right: Tim Evans arrives with a load of merchandis David Eccles' general merchandise store in Scofield, Utah, some in the 1880s. Eccles' chain of Utah stores was the beginning large financial institution that was to become known as First Sect Bank. (Photo by George Edward Anderson, BYU Photo Archi

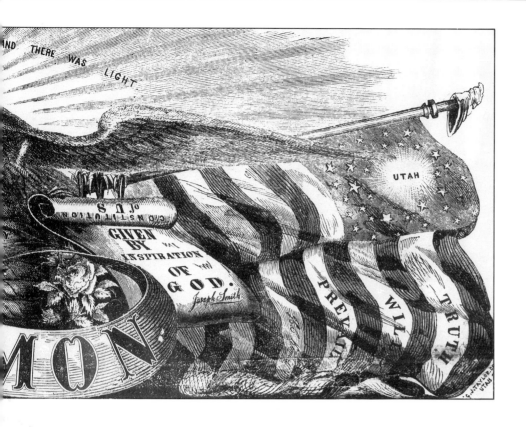

The Daniel H. Wells summer cottage on the south shore of t
Great Salt Lake near Black Rock (shown in the background)
pictured sometime in the 1870s, when the lake is high and surroun
Black Rock. Wells was an early civic leader among the Mormons
Nauvoo, was converted to Mormonism, commanded the Nauv
Legion, and served in the First Presidency with Brigham Your
(Photo by Charles W. Carter, LDS Historical Department)

The Johann Huber family of Haag am Hausrück, Mormon pione
in Austria at the turn of the century.

ol. Patrick Conner, military commander of the federal troops at
ort Douglas, was the first to recognize the value of mineral deposits
Utah. In 1862, men under his command mined for silver and gold
the mountains east of Salt Lake City, marking the start of Utah's
h legacy for precious metals. (Photo by Charles W. Carter, LDS
urch Historical Department)

Mormon family living in a log cabin with a sod roof is photo-
phed by Union Pacific Railroad photographer Andrew Joseph
ssell at Echo Junction in 1868. The photograph, which purport-
illustrates the Mormon practice of polygamy, is controversial,
ever, since Russell is suspected of staging the scene as a photo
stration rather than taking a photograph of a real situation. (Photo
Andrew Joseph Russell, Oakland Museum)

Farmers harvest grain near Chalk Creek in the 1880s in another artistic photograph by George Beard. (Photo by George Beard, BYU Ph[ ]
Archives)

railroad track bed has been graded through Echo Canyon in 1868, waiting for crews to lay the steel rails. (Photo by Andrew Joseph ssell, The Oakland Museum)

posite left, top: An Overland Stage waits for passengers on East mple Street (Main Street) in downtown Salt Lake City in the 0s. Stagecoach transportation was the chief mode of public trans- tation before the railroad was completed. (Photo by Charles W. ter, LDS Church Historical Department)

posite left, bottom: A Wells Fargo stage, loaded with passengers, out to embark on a trip west sometime around 1868. Completion he transcontinental railroad in 1869 spelled doom for the stage- ch method of interstate transportation. (Photo by Charles W. ter, LDS Church Historical Department)

Overleaf, pages 182–183: East shakes hands with the West at Pro- montory Point on May 10, 1869, at the driving of the Golden Spike, which marked completion of America's first transcontinental rail- road. Russell's view, said to be among the greatest news photographs of all time, shows Central Pacific's engine, "Jupiter," meeting Union Pacific's "No. 119" at Promontory, Utah. UP's chief engineer, Gren- ville M. Dodge, shakes hands with Central Pacific's Samuel S. Mon- tague, signaling completion of the world's engineering marvel of the century. (Photo by Andrew Joseph Russell, Oakland Museum)

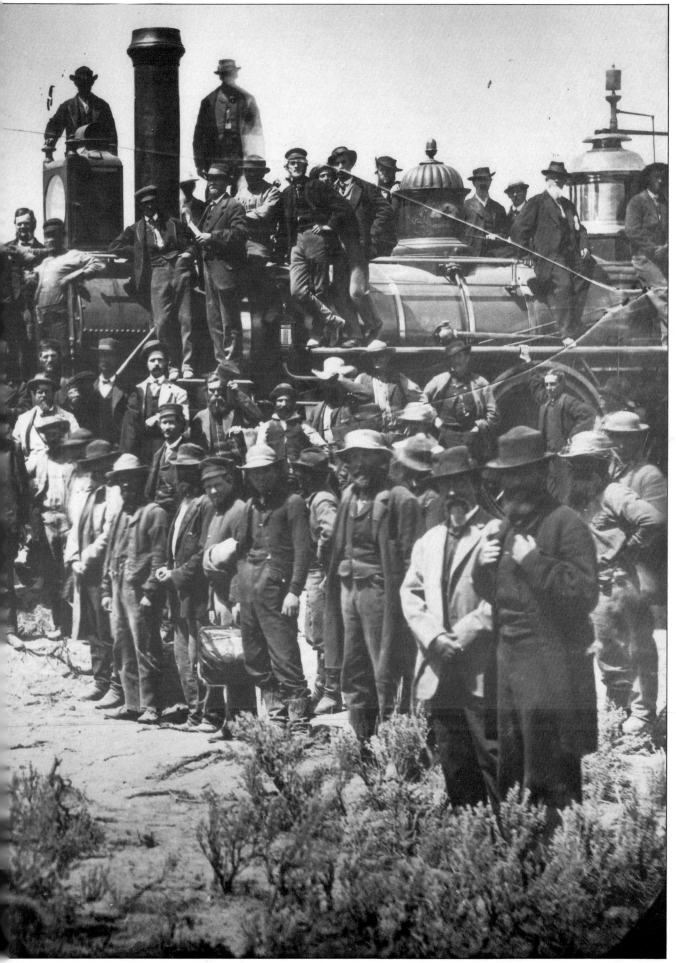

Opposite left, top: Lovenia Beard bathes her children in a washtub in the family home in Coalville, circa 1900. (Photo by George Beard, BYU Photo Archives)

Opposite left, bottom left: George Beard's wife, Lovenia, quietly sews near a window in Coalville in the 1880s. (Photo by George Beard, BYU Photo Archives)

Opposite left, bottom right: One of George Beard's sons displays a mess of fish taken from a pristine mountain stream in the High Uinta Mountains, which the artist-photographer was among the first to explore. (Photo by George Beard, BYU Photo Archives)

A patina of snow covers the foliage and landscape at Chalk Creek near Coalville, Utah, in an 1880s photograph taken by artist George Beard. The rural Mormon merchant took photographs to help in his oil painting, but a century later his photos are of as much value as his oils. (Photo by George Beard, BYU Photo Archives)

Members of an 1880s Beard exploration party scramble over the rocks atop a mountain peak in the High Uinta Mountains. In the distance is one of the highest peaks in the unique range, possibly King's Peak, 13,498 feet above sea level. (Photo by George Beard, BYU Photo Archives)

The Sevier County clerk and his deputy make entries in the public records of the rural, central Utah region, circa 1895. (Adams Collection, BYU Photo Archives)

: Utah secretary of state and an assistant work in their office in the state office building sometime before statehood in the 1890s. (Photo Heber Thomas, Oliver Collection, BYU Photo Archives)

posite left, top: The pioneer-built Social Hall in downtown Salt
e City was the first theater and center for entertainment in the
rmon settlement. It was built in the early 1850s and stood for
rly a century before being torn down. This photo shows how it
ked before its demolition. (Photo by Albert Wilkes, Utah His-
cal Society)

posite left, bottom: The Salt Lake Theater, shown here under
struction in 1861, was destined to become world famous, a center
heatrical performance in western America. It was completed in
2 and stood for nearly 70 years. (Photo Collection, Pioneer Vil-
, Lagoon, Utah)

Overleaf, pages 192–193: Members of the Castle Gate Choir pause
at the campgrounds at Soldier Summit in 1895 on their way to a
singing engagement, possibly a Mormon General Conference in Salt
Lake City. (Photo by George Edward Anderson, BYU Photo Archives)

A Mormon ward choir sings a number on the steps of their meeting house in Emery County, Utah, circa 1895. (Photo by George Edwa Anderson, BYU Photo Archives)

196

h's first symphony orchestra, the Salt Lake Symphony, performs in the Mormon Tabernacle in 1892, the year of its organization. Music mportant to the Mormon culture. (Photo by Charles Ellis Johnson, BYU Photo Archives)

posite left, top: A photograph taken sometime around 1865–
6 shows detail of the unique construction of the Mormon Tab-
cle. Rawhide and wooden pegs were used to lash the thick
ers together to create an acoustically sound but large meeting
se. (Photo by C. R. Savage, Savage photo album, BYU Photo
hives)

osite left, bottom: The foundation of the Mormon Temple rises
tone by stone in the foreground, with the completed Tabernacle
e background, in this 1867 photograph taken shortly after the
ed building was completed. (Photo by Charles W. Carter, LDS
orical Department Carter Collection)

DEPARTURE OF THE
F.R. CHICA

198

Members of the 350-voice Mormon Tabernacle Choir get ready to board trains in Salt Lake City on their way to perform at the Columbian Exposition at the 1893 World's Fair in Chicago. (Photo by Charles Ellis Johnson, BYU Photo Archives)

Opposite right, top: Joseph Ridges and his wife relax on the porc of their modest home in Salt Lake City. Ridges designed the hug wooden organ that has filled the Mormon Tabernacle with mus for more than a century. (Photo by Charles Ellis Johnson, BY Photo Archives)

Opposite right, bottom: At age 20, Alexander Schreiner, a native Nuremberg, Germany, sits at the organ console in the Mormo Tabernacle. He has just been appointed organist in the Tabernacl a position he would hold most of his life, for he would be numbere among the greatest organists in the world. (Utah Historical Societ

The Tabernacle Choir, backdropped by the huge Ridges organ, is photographed in 1896 at the celebration of Utah's statehood. The star of the organ signifies the addition of another star on the American flag. (Photo by Charles Ellis Johnson, BYU Photo Archives)

Overleaf, pages 202–203: Members of a Scottish clan in Utah have their picture taken sometime near the turn of the century. Because of Mormonism, Utah has always been the gathering place for a wide variety of ethnic groups from different nationalities. (Photo by Charles Ellis Johnson, BYU Photo Archives)

Opposite right: A montage of Church leaders, dating back to Jesu Christ, is displayed in this work of photographic art by Georg Edward Anderson of Springville, Utah. Known as "The Templ Floral Piece," it was a favorite decoration for the walls of Mormo homes during the administration of Mormon President John Taylo shown in the center with his counselors, George Q. Cannon, lef and Joseph F. Smith, right. (By George Edward Anderson, *Birth o Mormonism* album, Church Historical Department)

Participants in a Pioneer Day Parade, July 24, 1891, line up before marching through St. George, Utah. Mormons traditionally celebrate bo the Fourth of July (American Independence Day) and July 24th, the day pioneers arrived in Salt Lake Valley and began their Rocky Mounta settlement. (Photo by John Booth, Utah Historical Society)

Before the Temple was completed, sacred Mormon rites of celestial marriage and spiritual sealing were performed in the Endowment House which had been built on Temple Square to be used in the interim. (Utah Historical Society, John F. Bennett Collection)

Opposite right: Mormons get together for a summer picnic in Bowery, an open-air meeting place that was used for meetings p to the completion of the Tabernacle on Temple Square. (LDS Ch Historical Department)

Mormons gather on a snow-covered plot of ground April 6, 1853, to break ground for the Salt Lake Mormon Temple. The ceremonies marked the beginning of a 40-year construction project to erect their imposing granite "House of the Lord." (From an original daguerreotype, LDS Church Historical Department)

Overleaf, pages 210–211: Scaffolding still shrouds the Salt Lake Mormon Temple as crowds gather to celebrate the capping of the capstone on April 4, 1892. The Temple would be dedicated a year later at the Church's April Conference in 1893. (LDS Church Historical Department)

Above: Grant Brothers Stages bring visitors to Temple Squa[re] sometime in the 1880s, before the granite Temple was co[m]pleted. Stone for the building was quarried in Big Cottonwo[od] Canyon, south of Salt Lake City. (Photo by Charles Ellis Joh[n]son, BYU Photo Archives)

Opposite right, bottom left: A tiny figure stands on the t[op] spire where the Temple capstone would be lowered into plac[e.] (LDS Church Historical Department)

Opposite right, bottom right: An interior view of one roo[m] in the Salt Lake Temple shows rows of chairs where Mormo[ns] in good standing receive instructions on the sacred Temp[le] endowment. (Photo by Ralph Savage, LDS Church Historic[al] Department)

Overleaf, pages 214–215: Workmen install incandescent lig[ht] bulbs in the spires of the Salt Lake Temple in the 189[0s.] Photo of the southeast tower was taken from the highest e[ast] tower, with a hazy downtown Salt Lake City in the bac[k]ground. (LDS Church Historical Department)

Left: Workmen use sledge hammers to drill holes for splitti[ng] granite stones for use in the Mormon Temple. Stone for [the] Temple was quarried from Big Cottonwood Canyon, 20 mi[les] southeast of Salt Lake City. (Utah Historical Society, John [W.] Bennett Collection)

Left: President Wilford Woodruff, center, and counselors Georg[e] Q. Cannon, left, and Joseph F. Smith, right, pose for their forma[l] portrait at the time of the Temple dedication April 6, 1893. (Phot[o] by Charles Ellis Johnson, Utah Historical Society, John F. Benne[tt] Collection)

Opposite right: Joseph F. Smith, shown here at the time of th[e] Temple dedication, would later become the sixth President of th[e] Mormon Church. He served from 1901 to 1918. (Photo by Charl[es] Ellis Johnson, BYU Archives)

Overleaf, pages 216–217: Gleaming granite towers of the new[ly] completed Temple rise above Temple Square near turn of the ce[n]tury. It took pioneer craftsmen nearly four decades to complete th[e] building. (Photo by Charles Ellis Johnson, BYU Photo Archives)

Below: A flag drapes the south wall of the Salt Lake Temple in 18[9] in celebration of Utah's successful bid at statehood. (University [of] Utah Library Western Americana Collection)

THE AMERICANIZATION AND INTERNAL CONSOLIDATION OF MORMONISM: 1896–1951

The new era that officially began in 1896 with Utah becoming a state was characterized not only by the turning away from plural marriage and the integration of Utah into the American political system, but also by other changes. Early in his administration in 1903 the sixth President of the Church, Joseph F. Smith, a nephew of Joseph Smith, outlined to members the new church political posture, which has been reaffirmed periodically ever since. "The church (as such) does not engage in politics; its members belong to the political parties at their own pleasure." (Smith, Joseph F., 625)

Church statistics show a population of 205,000 in 1890 with the number increasing to 268,000 by the turn of the century. Mormons gradually accepted free enterprise capitalism in place of au-

tarky and experiments in cooperatives and communal economic orders, even though continued attention was paid to the care and welfare of the poor. A few Mormons, like Senator Reed Smoot, an apostle elected to the U.S. Senate, even began to gain respect and prestige on the American national scene. Gradually, the church rebounded from the dire financial straits it was in following the confiscation of its properties during the protracted polygamy conflict, primarily through a more faithful payment of tithes and offerings, loans, and prudent management. By 1907 it was free of debt. This firm financial foundation became a major basis for church prosperity in the second half of the twentieth century, a prerequisite for the ambitious worldwide building, missionary, and educational programs necessary for the exploding membership.

Opposite left: Utah children dress in patriotic costumes for an 1890s Independence Day celebration in Sanpete County. (Photo by George Edward Anderson, BYU Photo Archives)

Below: A homesteader near Lawrence, Emery County, Utah, lives a rugged life with his family in the desert southwest of Price. (Photo by George Edward Anderson, BYU Photo Archives)

At the same time, the pace of immigration began to slacken as church leaders, aware that the Mormon community in the Rocky Mountains was now large enough to be viable and setting their sights on the building of strong Mormon congregations in Europe, South America, and eventually Asia, began to discourage converts from coming to America. The age of the gathering was officially over, but not completely, especially among German-speaking Mormons. According to historian Douglas Alder's figures, before 1900 4,244—mostly Swiss—came to the United States. From then until 1939 another 4,852—mostly German—arrived. Because of the unique conditions of the uprooted in Germany after 1945 nearly 4,400 Germans, Austrians, and an occasional Swiss immigrated before 1958. (Alder, passim) Since 1960 the number has been apparently negligible.

In addition to the important processes of accommodation to American political and economic life and the gaining of a measure of respectability in society that characterized the Mormon experience in the early twentieth century, two other major related developments were taking place. The first was the internal transformation that Jan Shipps has eloquently described. In place of the quest for the establishment of the millennial kingdom of God in the here-and-now, Mormons now turned their considerable energies to the more transcendent achievement not only of eternal salvation but also of eternal progression through the strengthening of the faith and witness of each individual Mormon; for the church as a whole it meant a renewed commitment, expansion, and fervor to keeping the faith and doing missionary work. This combined with the ongoing internal consolidation within the church to form a strong foundation, making Mormon teachings and principles more understood and vital in the lives of church members.

At the same time new impetus was given to teaching within and strengthening the family units, closer adherence to the Word of Wisdom—the abstinence from alcohol, tobacco, tea, and coffee —a doctrine that outwardly put Mormons in stark contrast to the rest of the world of the first half of the twentieth century, but that over time has brought increased respect. Mormons were taught that it was possible and even desirable to live joyfully in this world, but also to prepare seriously for the next; the same principles of truth provided the basis for both. They were also to become better educated,

Above: Members of the Tidwell family pause from their daily labors to have their portrait taken in front of the log cabin they built on their homestead at Sunnyside, Utah. They were among the first settlers of that region of Carbon County, Utah. (Photo by George Edward Anderson, BYU Photo Archives)

Opposite right: Blacksmith Joseph Thurber works with sweat glistening on his brow as he shoes horses in Richfield, Utah, in the mid-1890s. (Photo by George Edward Anderson, BYU Photo Archives)

Overleaf, pages 224–225: Farm families wait in the courtyard of the Richfield Creamery in the 1890s to deliver milk and purchase dairy products. (Photo by George Edward Anderson, from a private collection)

to strive for and achieve a higher standard of living, to be more healthful, and to appreciate the countries and cultures wherever they lived. They could indeed be Saints anywhere in the world. Zion was no longer America or the West, but wherever in the world there were faithful Saints.

In 1930 the church celebrated its centennial. In that first century membership had grown from

(continued on page 246)

Above: Farm families top sugar beets at harvest time in central Utah sometime before the turn of the century. For many years sugar beets were a profitable cash crop for Mormon farmers. (Photo by George Edward Anderson, BYU Photo Archives)

Overleaf, pages 228–229: A mining family in Carbon County, Utah, gets ready to climb onto a wagon for a trip to town during coal boom of the 1890s. (Photo by George Edward Anderson, BYU Photo Archives)

Left: Farmers load pulp on wagons at one of the many sugar beet factories in central Utah (probably near Springville) at the turn of the century. The sugar beet culture in Utah dates back to the days of molasses making by the Mormon pioneers. (Photo by George Edward Anderson, BYU Photo Archives)

Four generations of the Franklin D. Richards family have their portrait taken. Franklin D., seated left, was ordained an apostle at 27, and later served as President of the Council of the Twelve Apostles before his death in 1899 in Ogden, Utah. (Photo by Charles Ellis Johnson, BYU Photo Archives)

Opposite right: Brigham H. Roberts, a member of the LDS Church Council of the Seventy, spoke up for Mormonism at the World Parliament of Religions in Chicago in 1893. He was elected to Congress in 1898 but was excluded from serving by fellow congressmen because he was a polygamist. Roberts later wrote a comprehensive history of the Mormon Church. (Photo by Charles Ellis Johnson, BYU Photo Archives)

Miss Liberty and her two young attendants get ready to celebrate American Independence Day at Ferron, Utah, sometime before the turn of the century. (Photo by George Edward Anderson, BYU Photo Archives)

surviving Pioneers of 1847 gather at the Pioneer Jubilee celebration on July 24, 1897, to have their portrait taken on the 50th anniversary their arrival in Utah. The photo was taken on Temple Square by Springville, Utah, photographer George Edward Anderson. (Photo by orge Edward Anderson, *Birth of Mormonism* album, LDS Historical Department)

Overleaf, pages 234–235: A crowd fills the intersection of Main and South Temple Streets in Salt Lake City at the unveiling of the Brigham Young and Pioneer Memorial Monument, which was dedicated July 20, 1897, kicking off the four-day Pioneer Jubilee Celebration. The monument was sculpted by Utah born artist Cyrus Dallin. (Photo by Charles R. Savage, from Savage scrapbook, BYU Photo Archives)

UNVEILING THE STATUE

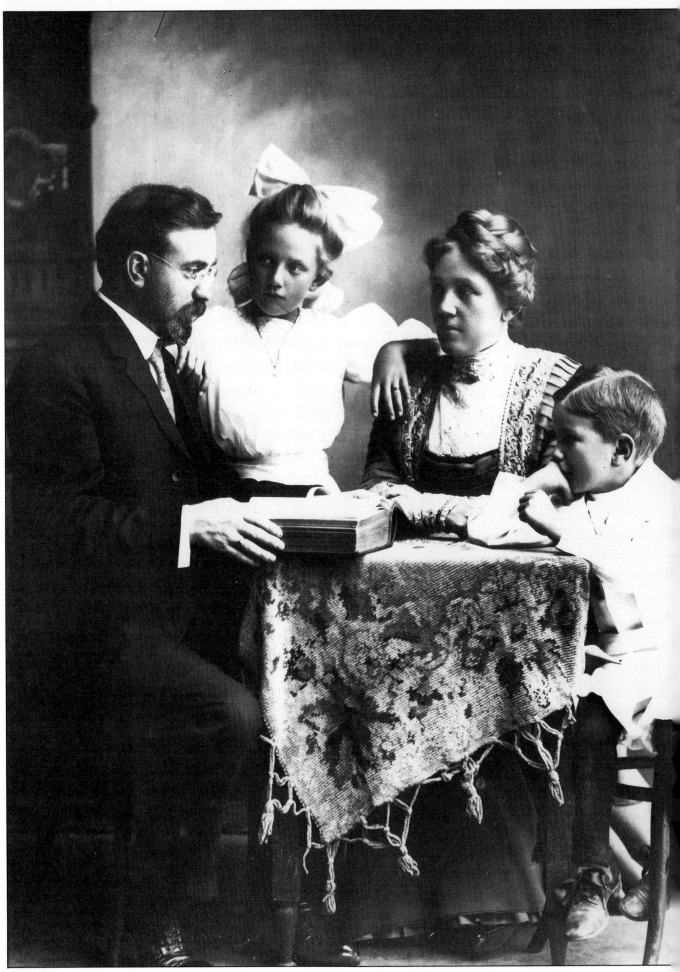

236

PAUL GILMORE AUDIENCE,
GRAND THEATRE, SALT LAKE, JAN. 1900.
JOHNSON.

...ominent American actor Paul Gilmore attracts a full house in the Salt Lake Theatre in January of 1900. The photo shows the elegant ...erior of the theater. (Photo by Charles Ellis Johnson, BYU Photo Archives)

...posite left: Mormon Apostle John A. Widtsoe reads the scriptures ...h his family during a regular Family Home Evening about 1912. ...rmons are encouraged by their leaders to hold regular family ...etings to study the Gospel and to discuss problems. (Photo by ...arles Ellis Johnson, BYU Photo Archives)

A school teacher in the little rural town of Koosharem in Sevier County gathers her brood of children for a photograph in front of the town's one-room, log school house. (Photo by George Edward Anderson, BYU Photo Archives)

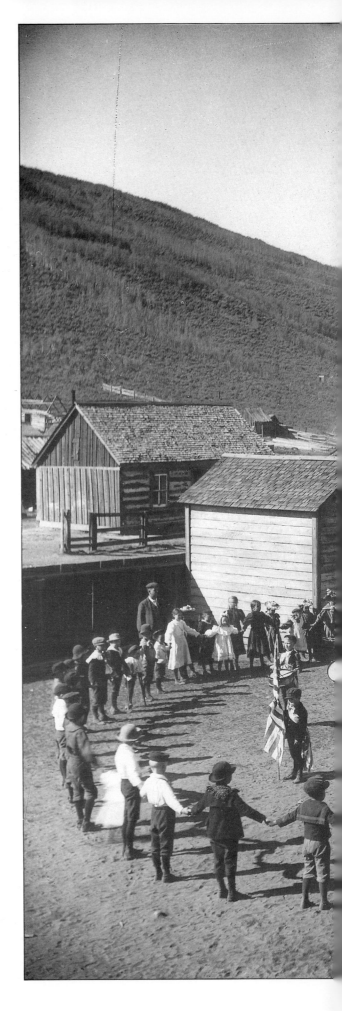

Right: Children form a circle around their drum and fife band at an Independence Day celebration at the elementary school in Scofield, Utah, in 1900. (Photo by George Edward Anderson, BYU Photo Archives)

Utah roadways at the turn of the century were mostly undeveloped and primitive, a challenge to automobile owners. Here, motorists dressed in traditional "dusters" attempt to clear the rugged roadway for their Maxwell to pass. (Photo by Wallace Bransford, BYU Photo Archives)

Left: The Maxwell Automobile Company built and marketed its world famous Maxwell in Salt Lake City. The vehicle for many years was among the most popular and durable on American roads. (Photo by Charles Ellis Johnson, BYU Photo Archives)

Opposite left: Mormon missionaries walk the streets in Jerusalem in 1904. Latter-day Saints expanded their religion by sending young Mormons around the world to preach their Gospel. (Photo by Charles Ellis Johnson, BYU Photo Archives)

This page, top: David Oman McKay, who was ordained an apostle at 32, visits the Great Wall of China in 1921 on a tour to establish missions around the world. He would later become president of the LDS Church and under his leadership would expand Mormonism throughout the globe. (Photo by Hugh Cannon, McKay Collection, LDS Historical Department) This page, bottom: Elders David O. McKay and Hugh Cannon conduct a Mormon conference in Tahiti in a huge circus tent. The two leaders visited Polynesian Mormons while on a world tour in 1921. (McKay Collection, LDS Historical Department)

Demonstrators rally in downtown Provo in 1910 in support of the seating of re-elected U.S. Senator Reed Smoot, a Mormon. The demonstration was aimed at Frank J. Cannon, editor of the *Salt Lake Tribune*, who had written a slanderous editorial and a series of magazine articles against Smoot and the Mormons. (Photo by Thomas C. Larson, BYU Photo Archives)

six to 672,488. Seventy-two percent of all Mormons still lived in the Intermountain West of Utah, Idaho, and Arizona; most continued to live in a rural setting with its agricultural economic base. But the dispersion had begun with significant Mormon congregations developing in Los Angeles and, later in the 1930s, in New York and Washington, D.C. Missionaries serving in Europe were instructed to continue to discourage Mormon emigration to America.

The church had also gone through the First World War where, for the first time, members had fought across from each other. A year or two after 1930 the full brunt of the Depression descended upon Saints everywhere; the church's response was an example of its "new" approach to dealing with the temporal problems of this world while keeping its sights firmly on eternity.

The symbol of the church in transition was its seventh President, Heber J. Grant. For twenty-seven years, from 1918 to 1945—longer than any other president except Brigham Young—Grant guided the church into the new era. Where his predecessor Joseph F. Smith had been embattled in defense of the church by non-Mormons and anti-Mormons in Utah and the United States, Grant soon gained considerable respect and even admiration for himself and the Mormon in the American community. He was the first Mormon President born in Utah—in 1856—and had been raised by a widowed mother who had performed menial labor in order to provide for her family. Grant had enjoyed, as a contemporary, Bryant S. Hinckley, wrote, "the advantages of poverty." (Hinckley, 702)

As a young man he became a successful businessman in an age in America when success in business meant power and respectability. "It is only fair to assume," a friend wrote in 1931, "that if he had continued to devote his time and great talents to the accumulation of wealth, he would not only have amassed a fortune, but would have found a place among the financial magnates of the world." (*Ibid*) Rather he chose to devote his life to church service. Still, the respect he gained rebounded to the benefit of the church in an era when it too was gaining a measure of respectability as a Christian faith.

Above: Major Hugh B. Brown, right, trains Canadian soldiers for duty in World War I. Brown would later be ordained an apostle in the LDS Church and would serve in the First Presidencies of two presidents. (LDS Historical Department)

Right: Major Joshua Reuben Clark, Jr., seated right, was among many Mormon young men who served in the armed forces of the United States during two World Wars. After serving as a commissioned officer in World War I, Clark served the United States as ambassador to Mexico. Ultimately, he was ordained an apostle in the LDS Church and served in the First Presidencies of two presidents. (BYU Photo Archives)

Grant became a local church leader at age 24 and one of the Quorum of Twelve Apostles two years later in 1880. He had grown up in pioneer Utah, had personally experienced the polygamy struggles and had headed a church mission to open up Japan to missionary work in 1901. From 1904 to 1906 he presided over all of the church's missions in Europe. To his associates and contemporaries, he was a great leader ideally suited for his time. An energetic man, he balanced a deep spirituality and conviction about Mormon teachings with common sense. Though deprived of much formal education, he had educated himself and became a lifelong patron and advocate of education for all Mormons. It is inconceivable that later Mormon attainments in education could have been achieved without this impetus. He believed in and taught Joseph Smith's Articles of Faith to all who would listen, especially on his European trip in 1937. He encouraged Mormons to keep their health laws and to pay their tithing, both for their spiritual as well as temporal well-being. Grant stoutly defended the separation of church and state and helped bring Mormons more fully into the American political order. But his major concern, as with his predecessors, remained the continued spread of Mormonism throughout the world. In a conference address in April 1927 he told assembled Mormons: "I want to emphasize that we as a people have one

supreme thing to do and that is to call upon the world to repent of sin, to come to God. And it is our duty above all others to go forth and proclaim the gospel of the Lord Jesus Christ, the restoration again to the earth of the plan of life and salvation." (*LDS Conference Reports*, 175)

If Grant's administration had begun in an age of prosperity, it was soon engulfed by the woes of the Depression, which affected Mormons as much as anyone. In 1930 there were more than 6,000 people, mostly Mormons, looking for work in Salt Lake City. (Alexander and Allen, 201) In 1934, Utah had 206 persons per thousand on relief, the fourth highest state in the United States. A year

Below: Trolley tracks intersect at Main and South Temple streets in downtown Salt Lake City shortly after the turn of the century. In the background is the newly completed Union Pacific Building. UP financiers put up the money for a sophisticated transit system in Salt Lake City that for many years was among the most advanced in the world. (Photo by Charles Ellis Johnson, BYU Photo Archives)

Opposite right: Mormon President Heber J. Grant, center, flanked by counselors J. Reuben Clark, left, and David O. McKay, right, pause on the steps of the Church Administration Building to be photographed. Picture was probably taken about the time Clark and McKay were sustained as Grant's counselors in 1934. (LDS Historical Department)

J. Reuben Clark

Heber J. Grant

David O. McKay

later a church-wide survey showed that almost 18 percent of the membership (88,460 persons) were receiving church or government help. (Allen and Leonard, 519–520)

The church immediately began to organize to take better care of poor and unemployed Mormons. The Church Welfare Program, a comprehensive plan to care for those in need, was put in place in 1936. Land was purchased where food crops could be raised and canned to be given to the unemployed or needy. Women canned food, made bedding, and sewed clothes. Jobs were found or created in make-work projects; those who worked and those who were unable could obtain food, clothing, and fuel at the church's storehouses. "By 1938 approximately twenty-two thousand Latter-day Saints had been taken off federal relief rolls and more than thirty thousand others had received some kind of aid. Private employment had been found for an additional twenty-four hundred." (*Ibid*, 523) This Mormon Welfare Program became so successful that it was able, under the direction of the current President, Ezra Taft Benson, then an apostle, to send approximately 140 railroad carloads of food and clothing valued at two million dollars to war-torn Europe (110 to Germany) between 1946 and 1949. In 1947 alone 6,872 persons, mostly Germans, were helped. (*Ibid*, 553; Koontz) More than a few German Mormons and non-Mormons attributed the sparing of their lives to the commodities the Church Welfare Program was able and willing to provide. This same program has been lauded from that day to this by statesmen from around the world.

The concern with the Depression gave way in the latter half of the 1930s to the threat of war. As noted earlier, during the inter-war period, especially the early 20s, Germany had produced a surprising number of Mormon converts (7,776 from 1920 to 1924) so that by 1930 Germany had more Mormons (11,306) than any other country except the United States, and that in spite of continued emigration. (Scharffs, xiv) It was little wonder, then, that the church was vitally interested in its missionary work and in building up its congregation in Germany, as well as in other parts of the world,

A Mormon Relief Society president picks up goods for welfare recipients from a Regional Storehouse sometime in the late 1930s. The LDS Welfare Program set up a series of food and clothing storehouses to take care of the poor and needy. (LDS Church Historical Department)

and worked, after 1933, to get along with the new Hitler regime. In 1937 the church president, Heber J. Grant, visited Germany and encouraged Mormons to stay there, to be good citizens, and to keep the commandments. There were, by 1938, many characteristics of the Nazi regime that church leaders found "detestable," but they tried diligently to protect their flock there and gain new members.

The war that soon became all too stark a reality again found Mormons being killed on both sides of the battle lines. The position toward the war taken by Latter-day Saints was spelled out in a statement given by the church's First Presidency at the semi-annual conference, October 4, 1940. It has been the major document on war and peace in the ensuing four decades:

The meeting of the Saints in this General Conference finds the world still war torn. Millions of the Lord's children are suffering and mourning. All the woes and misery that attend armed conflict are spending their force upon them. . . .

Our brethren and sisters are found on both sides of this terrible struggle. On each side they are bound to their country by all the ties of blood, relationship and patriotism.

As always happens in such cases, each side claims to believe it is in the right. Each claims to feel it is fighting for its very existence. As the war progresses in its cruelty and horror, each may come to

aim at the complete subjugation or extermination of the other.

This would be an inhuman and unrighteous purpose. . . .

The Saints on either side have no course open but to support that government to which they owe allegiance. But their prayers should go up day and night that God will turn the hearts of their leaders toward peace, that the curse of war may end.

God is not pleased with war, or with the wickedness which always heralds it. . . .

The hearts of all the Saints are torn with grief over the sufferings of their brethren and sisters who are taking part in this struggle. So, for the Saints this is a fratricidal conflict. They so mourn over it. . . .

To those Saints who are stricken by this great tragedy, we say live righteously, pray constantly, and the Lord will answer as your faith and work and His all-wise purposes allow Him.

To those whose wickedness has brought this strife and turmoil, we say repent lest the Lord shall smite you in His wrath. He will not hold you guiltless of the innocent blood of your fellowmen. (Clark 6:115–117)

The statement concluded with a prayer for the banishment of hate from the souls of men ". . . that sanity shall again assert its sway, and that love shall fill the hearts of men even to overflowing."

But it was not to be. Like everyone else the Saints were directly affected by the war as hundreds of church members lost their lives.

Left: A crowd gathers in front of a modest home in the streets of Meissen, Germany, on January 11, 1928, to commemorate the 100th anniversary of the birth of Mormon educator Karl Maeser, at the place of his birth. (BYU Photo Archives)

Below: Missionaries evacuated from Germany in August of 1939 just before World War II with Elder Joseph Fielding Smith of the Quorum of the Twelve and his wife, Jesse Evans Smith, in Copenhagen, Denmark.

Left: The elegant Saltair Resort on the south shore of the Great Salt Lake stood like a huge Moorish castle for many years before the lake abandoned her and she burned to the ground. This photo shows the resort in its heyday after World War I, when the lake was at a high-water mark. (Photo by Albert Wilkes, Utah Historical Society)

Overleaf, pages 254–255: A couple and their cat enjoy an elegantly furnished home in Salt Lake City sometime after World War I. Utah lifestyles had moved out of a spartan pioneer existence and into the modern age. (Photo by Heber Thomas, Pioneer Village, Lagoon Amusement Park)

Overleaf, pages 258–259: The most prominently situated building in the Salt Lake Valley, the classically styled Utah State Capitol, overlooks Utah's capital city. This photo, taken sometime in the 1920s, shows the snow-capped Wasatch Mountains in the background and the sprawling growth in the city founded by the Mormons. (Photo by Albert Wilkes, Utah Historical Society)

Opposite left, top: Mormon general authorities gather at the construction site in Salt Lake City in 1914 to lay the cornerstone for a Church administrative office building on South Temple Street. Heads are bowed in prayer as the cornerstone is dedicated before a granite block, right, is lowered into place over a metal box containing artifacts of that time in the Church's history. (Photo by Albert Wilkes, Utah Historical Society)

Opposite left, bottom: The new Church administrative office building was completed in 1917 and at the time was said to be one of the finest examples of Greek architecture west of the Mississippi River. (Photo by Albert Wilkes, Utah Historical Society)

Overleaf, pages 262–263: A delivery truck loads supplies at the Bishops' Salt Lake Regional Storehouse sometime during the Great Depression of the 1930s. Economic hardships among Mormons led to the establishment of the model LDS Church Welfare Program to supply help to the poor and needy. (LDS Church Historical Department)

An aerial view taken in the 1920s shows Brigham Young University when it consisted of only three buildings on a hill and an athletic field north of the campus. (BYU Photo Archives)

Above: David O. McKay, pictured here about the time of his world mission tour, would eventually become President of the LDS Church and would be loved by Mormons and non-Mormons alike around the world. Under his leadership, Mormonism would move into the modern age. (Photo by Heber Thomas, Pioneer Village, Lagoon Amusement Park)

Left: David O. McKay, at the rostrum, conducts the April, 1936, General Conference for the LDS Church in Salt Lake City. Seated directly behind him are President Heber J. Grant and other apostles. To the left are members of the famed Mormon Tabernacle Choir. (Photo by Bill Shipler, LDS Historical Department)

Below: General authorities of the LDS Church and their wives take time out of their busy schedules to enjoy a swim at Saltair Resort sometime in the late 1920s. Included in the photo are, far left, Joseph Fielding Smith, and far right, George Albert Smith, who would later serve as Presidents of the Church. (LDS Church Historical Department)

THE AGE OF INTERNATIONALISM AND GROWTH: 1951–1989

With the end of the war Mormons returned with increased vigor to their by now well-established goals: the spiritual strengthening of each other toward what the Apostle Paul had called "the perfecting of the Saints"; the living of Christ-like lives in an expanding, secular world; the re-invigoration of the missionary work largely curtailed by the war; and the building of new temples to bring vicarious salvation to the dead. Yet, by 1950 the church was still largely an American church, although the man who became president in 1951, David O. McKay, had an international orientation that would successfully build on the work of his predecessors to catapult the church over the next two decades into the international arena. Indeed, as historians James B. Allen and Glen Leonard have written, the dominant themes of Mormon history since 1950 have been its growth and internationalization. (Allen and Leonard, 561 ff.) In addition, the church has become much more urban, more educated, more middle class, and more affluent. Both the church and its members have become more known and respected throughout the world, but especially in the United States, have vastly increased their membership and presence in Latin America and Asia, and most recently have

begun more vigorous proselyting in Africa.

The figures for 1950 provide a starting point for understanding this period of internationalization and modernization. Church membership stood at 1,111,314; the rate of growth had been 28 or 29 percent for the past three decades of the 20s, 30s and 40s the lowest since the difficult days of the 1880s. More than 950,000 Mormons lived in the United States and most of those in the inter-mountain region. Canada had some 16,000; Germany (West and East), 15,000; Britain, 6,000; New Zealand, nearly 12,000; and Mexico, 7500, to mention only the top six ranking countries. (Scharffs, xiv) By contrast, in 1980, some representative figures illustrate the international thrust. There were 139,000 Mormons in Asia with 57,000 in Japan, 41,000 in the Philippines, and 22,000 in Korea. Mormons have also succeeded in gaining a number of converts in Taiwan, but only a few in India and none in the People's Republic of China. (Stark, 24)

Between 1960 and 1980 the Mormon membership in South America jumped from fewer than 10,000 to 368,000; in Mexico from 18,000 to 241,000; and in Great Britain from 6,000 to 90,000. Increases for continental Western Europe were not as great, as

Above: LDS President David O. McKay makes a strong point during a talk at Mormon Conference in the Tabernacle in the 1950s. President McKay served his church most of his life, including the last two decades as president. His service stretched from the horse and buggy days of transportation through the modern jet age. (Photo by J.M. Heslop, *The Deseret News*)

Opposite left: A Mormon Explorer Scout troop makes its way down the Escalante River in a desert wilderness area in southeastern Utah in 1958. Mormons have been supporters of the Boy Scout program since its inception in 1910. (Photo by Nelson Wadsworth)

church membership records show approximately 100,000 members lived west of the line separating the West and East blocs and another 4,000 in countries under communist rule. Most of these live in the German Democratic Republic where thriving Mormon congregations in existence before World War II have been not only preserved but also strengthened by the two generations of children that have chosen to remain "true to the faith." There the temple dedicated in 1985 in Freiberg near Dresden is a visual symbol of the vigor and dedication of the Mormon community in the German Democratic Republic.

When David O. McKay became President of the Church, it was already poised for a "great leap" forward. McKay was well prepared for his role, which would emphasize not only the international growth but also the ability to educate, especially at the college level, this burgeoning population, mostly of young people.

McKay was himself an educator and the first Mormon President to have gained a college education (valedictorian of his class at the University of Utah). His counselors and associates were also well educated and understood well the growing importance of education for the modern world.

McKay appears to have always had a broad perspective on the world. He was proud of his Scottish heritage, which had been reaffirmed in a mission to Scotland just before the turn of the century, in 1897. But this international outlook was heightened by a round-the-world trip he took at the request of church leadership. This trip was the fulfillment of a prophecy made about him when a teenage boy, with his friend, Hugh J. Cannon, a few years later, the mission president in Switzerland and Germany, in 1929. Later during his presidency he was responsible for the construction of the first temples outside of the United States and Canada—in Switzerland, London, and New Zealand—and instituted an enormous program for building chapels for church worship around the world. Allen and Leonard have written that the church ". . . erected and dedicated 1,350 chapels, schools, and welfare buildings between 1946 and 1955, at an average cost of $90,000 each, and the chapels built in that period constituted more than half of the chapels then in use. In 1955 alone the church spent $18,700,000 (which amounted to over half of the total church budget) on buildings from its general funds. Another $11,300,000 was contributed directly by members." (Allen and Leonard, 572) By comparison, in April 1985 President Gordon B. Hinckley of the First Presidency reported that more than 900 chapels, ranging from an estimated $300,000 to $2 million, were currently under construction.

McKay made similar commitments to church education, especially to higher education. Symbolic has been the growth of Brigham Young University. In 1951 the university enrolled 4,510 students; by 1960 the number had doubled. The faculty had grown from 196 to 502 and a dozen new buildings had been erected on the hill where the first building—Maeser—had been dedicated in 1911. By around 1970 student enrollment had jumped to an established limit of 25,000, where it has remained. Similar growth has taken place at the BYU-Hawaii campus and at Ricks College in Idaho, a two-year school founded in the nineteenth century that in 1986 had an enrollment of more than 7,000.

Opposite right, top and bottom: The Mormon Pavilion at the New York World's Fair in 1963–1964 represented a bold effort on the part of Mormon leaders to inform the public about their religion. Millions of people visited the pavilion for a better understanding of Mormonism. The Mormon Pavilion was situated close to the Flushing line of the subway entrance to the fair and was among the first displays encountered by visitors in 1963–1964. (Photo by Nelson Wadsworth)

Below: An old stone structure still remained of the Vauxhall meeting place in Great Britain in 1958 when it was photographed by *Deseret News* photographer J. Malin Heslop. The building served as a chapel for Mormon services in England in 1840, when Mormonism was first preached in the British Isles. The building has since been torn down. (Photo by J.M. Heslop, *The Deseret News*)

Above: When this photograph was taken in 1958, the John Benbow Farm at Frome's Hill, England, looked much like it did when Morm
Missionary Wilford Woodruff preached here for the first time March 5, 1840, establishing the roots of Mormonism in England.

Opposite right: Gravestones mark the pioneer cemetery at Winter Quarters, Nebraska, where thousands of Mormon Pioneers were bur
before the Latter-day Saints migrated westward to Utah.

Below: An LDS chapel stands in Preston, England, where Mormon congregations first got started in 1840. In that year, Mormon missionar
including Brigham Young, converted several thousand English people and began a steady migration from Great Britain to Utah.

(Photos by J.M. Heslop, *The Deseret News*)

Similar strides were made in the expansion of the missionary program. Most Mormons who were church members in the 1950s and 1960s will remember David O. McKay for his admonition "Every member a missionary." However, many more missionaries were called; by 1965 there were 12,000 missionaries serving. That number rose to 16,000 by 1973.

In no part of the world did membership grow as much in the 70s as in Latin America. From 18,700 in 1960 the Mormon population grew to 135,000 within the decade. Vigorous new stakes (dioceses) with the full programs of the church were established from Mexico in the north to Argentina in the south. Growth was so rapid that it was difficult to train and provide adequate lay church leadership for the congregations that were being formed virtually every week. The church also established elementary schools in some of these countries where public education was unavailable.

This enormous post-war expansion of Mormonism did not come cheaply. Whatever wealth the church presently has—a topic of some speculation—dates from this era. Mormons, especially in the United States, benefited from the post-war years of prosperity that, together with the faithfulness of the Saints in tithe paying and, to a much lesser extent, sound investments, helped to provide the funds to make the expansion and consolidation of the Kingdom more possible.

It was also during the McKay years that a more positive image of Mormons in the general public, especially in America, began to emerge. At the same time the image of Mormons among some secularized intellectuals was one of fanatic fundamentalism as they adhered to literal interpretation of scripture, the belief in a personal God, the efficacy of prayer, and traditional standards of Christian conduct. This was primarily a product of increased contact with Mormons as they began

Scoutmaster Hugh Baird of Provo, Utah, takes some time on a trail in the High Uinta Primitive Area in the Utah mountain wilderness to instruct his troop on survival in the outdoors. The backdrop is the world-famous Naturalist Basin. (Photo by Nelson Wadsworth)

Mormon youths carry buckets and ladders through a Church Welfare apple orchard in Payson, Utah, getting ready to harvest a crop for their Church. The young people donate their time without compensation as a contribution to welfare service. (Photo by Nelson Wadsworth)

to spread throughout the nation and the world. More and more people began to discover that Mormons had neither horns nor more than one wife, and that they were good neighbors and friends. Occasionally, some Mormons alienated themselves with overbearing attempts to "convert" their neighbors but, in general, respect was growing. One non-Mormon Viennese lawyer enjoyed teasing his Mormon friends. "They were nice people," he said, "but their timing was poor. They practiced polygamy in the nineteenth century when most other people were opposed to it. Now in the twentieth they no longer were engaging in it while the world was condoning a multiplicity of different liaisons."

There was some truth in it as Mormons continued to teach the same theology—without polygamy—that they had from the beginning: absolute fidelity to the Ten Commandments as well as to the teaching of Jesus Christ in the New Testament and the Book of Mormon.

Respect for Mormons was also manifest by the attention given to McKay and others by U.S. Presidents; the wide influence and recognized excellence of the Tabernacle Choir; the example of Ezra Taft Benson as Secretary of Agriculture under President Dwight Eisenhower; the success of the Church Welfare Program and much more favorable publicity by the press. By the 1960s America was beginning to pay Mormonism a compliment by taking it seriously.

The same was not true for Western Europe. There the church in 1960 was actually "starting over" following the wars and the long period of emigration. The appearance of temples and chapels in Europe—Bern and London—gave European Mormons visible signs that the church was there to stay as much as it was in America. By 1960 Europeans had little economic motivation for emigration and most Mormons came to believe that it was as possible to live the life of a Saint in Stutt-

gart or Southampton or Stockholm as in Salt Lake City. The Mormon version of "eternal recurrence," the continual starting over following emigration, was over and the foundations were being laid for the second- and third-generation Mormon families in Europe upon which the permanent church there could be built. Moreover, for the first time, Mormons began to gain significant numbers of converts in Roman Catholic areas as the secularization of these societies accelerated. Missionary work became more productive in France and Austria, and new missions were subsequently opened up in Italy, Ireland, Spain, and Portugal. Gradually in all European countries Mormon congregations became less dominated by blue-collar workers as second- and third-generation Mormons began to attend

Children at Primary Children's Hospital in Salt Lake City display their skills at finger-painting. The modern hospital receives children with difficult medical problems from all over the world. (Photo by J.M. Heslop, *The Deseret News*)

A Primary teacher instructs a group of LDS children in fundamentals of the Gospel of Jesus Christ. Mormons believe in giving children a firm foundation in applying Gospel principles in their lives. (Photo by J.M. Heslop, *The Deseret News*)

Members of a Ward in Pioneer Stake, Salt Lake City, bow their heads in prayer at the opening of a meeting sometime in the 1960s. Similar Mormon congregations meet all over the world. (Photo by J.M. Heslop, *The Deseret News*)

universities or find success in a broader range of professional and business activities. In addition, more middle class people in all countries began to investigate and join the church.

The death of David O. McKay did not change the direction or dynamism of the church. His successor, Joseph Fielding Smith, grand nephew of Joseph Smith, the founding prophet, had helped Mormons understand their theology for over fifty years. He also presided over the establishment of holding general conferences outside of Utah, the first of which was held in Manchester, England, with a later one in Munich. In Manchester, in 1970, Smith, a long time advocate of "gathering" to Utah and the United States, expressed the new reality:

We are members of a world church . . .

The day is long since past when informed people think of us as a strange group in the tops of the Rocky Mountains in America. . . . We are coming of age as a church and as a people. We have attained

the stature and strength that are enabling us to fulfill the commission given us by the Lord through the Prophet Joseph Smith that we should carry the glad tidings to every nation and to all people. . . .

Thus the church is not an American church except in America. In Canada it is a Canadian church; in Australia it is an Australian church; and in Great Britain it is a British church. It is a world church; the gospel is for all men. (Quoted in Allen and Leonard, 598)

The completion of a new twenty-six-story church administration building in Salt Lake City with external murals of the world map became another visible symbol of the emerging world church.

Joseph Fielding Smith died in 1972 and his successor, Harold B. Lee, followed a year and a half later. Lee had been an apostle since 1940, had been a primary architect of the Welfare Plan and directed the far-reaching internal coordination and

Mormon Relief Society sisters share some knitting secrets at a meeting in Salzburg, Austria. (Photo by J.M. Heslop, *The Deseret News*)

presidency of the church. This modest, self-effacing common man, the son of Arizona pioneer stock, had hardly dreamed that someday he might become the senior apostle and therefore, according to tradition and usage, the new president of the church. Most, including himself, expected him to be a caretaker president, rather than the dynamic revolutionary he turned out to be. But the dramatic leadership was not long in coming. What followed was a twelve-year ministry that a close associate, Neal A. Maxwell, wrote could only be described by using "some superlatives." (Maxwell, 8)

Though he did not "look like a prophet," as was often said about the tall, stately McKay, Kimball soon became uniquely beloved to Mormons and others who knew him around the world. Business men, professionals, homemakers, academicians, laborers—people of every walk of life and in every culture—found a "special and discernible dimension of affection for and identification with [him]." (*Ibid.*) He radiated love and warmth, treated each person, especially social pariahs, as if they were God's special child, and sought in every way to cause all to live a life in the image of Christ, the life-style which he himself lived. His ability to transcend countless illnesses and numerous surgeries, ranging from throat cancer to open heart surgery to relieving pressure on his brain, and still lead a useful and productive life provided quiet encouragement for thousands.

Kimball was also singularly effective in helping those who had erred to find both the energy and the way to regain the self-esteem and dignity in a world of sin and degradation.

But beyond these powerful pastoral achievements he was a dynamic and revolutionary leader. At no time in the church's history did it grow so rapidly, especially through convert baptisms. When he became president at the end of 1973, church membership stood at 3,321,556; at the end of 1985, just two months after his death, the figure had risen to 5,920,000 with 65 percent in the United States and 35 percent outside. Some 225,000 Mormons live in Europe in 1986. The full-time missionary force reached 30,000 as many young women, in a Mormon version of the Feminist Revolution, joined the growing army of missionaries to teach Mormonism wherever they were sent. Missionaries were also better trained and better supervised. For the Mormons in the Kimball era, heeding the counsel

correlation reforms within the church in the 60s. Henceforth, Mormons would receive a more systematic and thorough education in scripture, theology, and practice at three levels: first as a child, then as a youth, and finally as an adult. The results of this improved understanding were greater devotion and activity on the part of Mormons in general.

Lee also perceived the need for the church to have its own international ambassador much as the Vatican had its own diplomatic corps. David Kennedy, a former Chicago banker, Secretary of the Treasury, and NATO ambassador, was later called in April 1974 to that position. His role became symbolic for the new vigorous outreach beginning in the early 1970s especially into countries in Eastern Europe and around the world where Mormons had up to that time been unable to proselyte.

The death of Harold B. Lee in December 1975, brought 80-year-old Spencer W. Kimball to the

of the prophet meant following his example to literally bring the message to everyone on the globe.

There were some new dimensions to the proselyting program. In August 1977, accompanied by Ambassador Kennedy, Kimball traveled to Poland to sign documents officially recognizing the church in that country and opening it up on a limited basis for proselyting. This was the first time a Mormon President had been behind the Iron Curtain. But it signalled something more. In place of the more strident anti-Communism of the post World War II era, he took a position of getting along with all governments in order to bring the transcendent message of salvation to more of the people of the world. Lacking interest in political matters, he seemed impatient to wait for the Communist governments to be changed, preferring to

Branch President Rudolf Weissenberger greets two Austrian Mormons at a Church conference in Salzburg in 1963. (Photo by J.M. Heslop, *The Deseret News*)

Mormon Relief Society members donate their time in a Welfare Cannery in Utah. Products are canned for the Bishops' Storehouses to stockpile food for the poor and the needy. (Photo by J.M. Heslop, *The Deseret News*)

Mormon Relief Society sist[ers] weave mats from native fibers [in] an LDS Church project in Tah[iti] South Pacific. Thousands of Po[ly]nesians accept Mormonism b[e]cause they believe the Book [of] Mormon to be a history of th[eir] ancestors. (Photo by J.M. Hesl[op] *The Deseret News*)

Edith Aumau and Sigolu Sa[p] admire the many tropical flowers [on] the grounds of the Mormon Te[m]ple in Hawaii in 1969. (Photo [by] J.M. Heslop, *The Deseret New[s]*)

rmon missionaries talk to peo-
on the streets of Seoul, South
rea. More than 30,000 mission-
s are abroad in many countries
he world to preach the Mor-
n message. (Photo by J.M. Hes-
, *The Deseret News*)

Polynesian Mormon in New
land displays one of his prize
s. (Photo by J.M. Heslop, *The
eret News*)

accept whatever opportunities they would grant to carry out the church's unique mission. Similarly, the church developed an ultra-modern communications network with which to maintain contact with its far-flung membership and to aid the missionary cause.

At the same time, the church did choose to speak out in 1981 against the deployment of the MX missile system in Utah and Nevada. The church could not reconcile putting such a system in a place from where they were trying "to carry the gospel of peace to the peoples of the earth;" it controverted the church's century-old primary mission. The statement then elaborated the concern:

> With the most serious concern over the pressing moral question of possible nuclear conflict, we plead with our national leaders to marshal the genius of the nation to find viable alternatives which will secure at an earlier date and with fewer hazards the protection from possible enemy aggression which is our common concern. ("LDS Church Leaders Oppose MX")

Some analysts in the United States and Europe believed the church's stand essentially killed the MX program. While the distinguished German journalist Theo Sommer approvingly called the matter to the attention of Germans, conservative columnist William F. Buckley lamented the statement by asking, "Who gave Mormons power to bar MX?" Aside from the significant moral issues involved, the responses were an interesting commentary on the influence the church had acquired in the world in recent years.

Another Mormon expression of love for fellow person was a special fast conducted on January 27, 1985 in behalf of those starving in Africa. As a result, some $6.4 million was turned over to the International Red Cross, CARE, and Catholic charities for distribution.

A combination of love and concern was embodied in the church's 1978 decision, under Kimball's leadership, to grant the power of priesthood authority for the first time to blacks. This revelation reaffirmed the continuous Mormon commitment to the church being led by divine revelation and represented the first significant doctrinal change since the abolition of polygamy in 1890. A substantial part of the text is as follows:

> . . . Aware of the promises made by the prophets and presidents of the church who have preceded us that at some time, in God's eternal plan, all of our brethren who are worthy may receive the priesthood, and witnessing the faithfulness of those from whom the priesthood has been withheld, we have pleaded long and earnestly in behalf of these, our faithful brethren, spending many hours in the upper room of the temple supplicating the Lord for divine guidance.

> He has heard our prayers, and by revelation has confirmed that the long-promised day has come when every faithful, worthy man in the church may receive the holy priesthood, with power to exercise its divine authority, and enjoy with his loved ones every blessing that flows therefrom, including blessings of the temple. Accordingly, all worthy male members of the church may be ordained to the priesthood without regard for race or color.

> . . . We declare with soberness that the Lord has now made known His will for the blessing of all His children throughout the earth who will hearken to the voice of His authorized servants, and prepare themselves to receive every blessing of the gospel. (*Doctrine and Covenants*, Official Declaration-2:293–294)

For the small but growing black Mormon community, it was, as Joseph Freeman, the first black to receive the priesthood, said, "something we've waited a long time for." So had many white Mormons. Throughout the church an overwhelming majority welcomed the change in policy and blacks into their congregations. A predicted wave of withdrawals failed to materialize.

For Spencer Kimball, the bringing of the full gospel around the world could not be accom-

Opposite right: Church President Spencer W. Kimball, left, chats with U.S. President Gerald Ford in the White House Rose Garden in Washington, D.C., on July 3, 1976, during the nation's Bicentennial Celebration. (Photo by Nelson Wadsworth)

plished without a comparable acceleration in temple building and temple attendance. Early in his administration a stately edifice in Washington, D.C., was dedicated; it was a symbol of Mormon presence in America. But thereafter the philosophy began to change; instead of bringing Mormons to larger more monumental structures as had been done in the past, the idea was to build more of them, make them smaller and more accessible to Mormons everywhere. They, too, are symbols of the expanding universal church. During the Kimball years, twenty-one temples were dedicated from Washington to Tokyo, from Santiago, Chile to Sydney, Australia, from Johannesburg to Freiberg in the German Democratic Republic. Additional temples have been announced or completed in Ecuador, Korea, Toronto, and Frankfurt, to mention only a few.

All of these have continued to the present day under Kimball's successor, Ezra Taft Benson; but he has also added his own unique emphasis and touch. He has challenged and inspired the worldwide Mormon community to read, study, and live by the teachings of the Book of Mormon like few prophets before him. It is not unlikely that this guidance will lead both to a deepened, spiritual rejuvenation among the faithful and to an increase in conversions where Mormons are permitted to proselyte. In 1988 the church gained new recognition and missionary opportunities in Hungary and the German Democratic Republic with the hope of similar breakthroughs in the Soviet sphere of influence. The Mormons are also pursuing these same objectives in countries of Asia and Africa which up to this point have been closed to them. Mormons are also being encouraged to focus more clearly on the worth and dignity of each individual person, and to attend to the strengthening of family ties through improved understanding between wives and husbands, parents and children. Mormon women overwhelmingly do not seek the right to the governing priesthood, but are looking to the church for guidance in their contemporary self-definition in a world in the midst of the Women's Revolution.

At the same time, the church, with its apotheosis of the family as an eternal institution, is also challenged to minister well to a growing number of single people and to those with less traditional lifestyles.

There is also some evidence that the church and its members are moving away from the religious isolationism of the past when they were persecuted not only by individuals and governments, but also by other Christian churches. Mormon interfaith cooperation has increased on both the international level, whose churches joined together to ameliorate the hunger of African peoples, and in local communities where cooperation has benefited the poor and the homeless. The church seems poised to turn itself out toward the world to an extent not yet experienced in its history.

The dynamism of the man and the age was also felt internally. New general authorities were added to keep up with worldwide leadership demand; the number of stakes offering the full program of the church to its members doubled; members were aided in their study of the scriptures by new study guides and helps; all were encouraged to adhere to the timeless Judeo-Christian moral values; parents and children were admonished to have regular weekly "home evenings," both to strengthen the family unit and to give all members a firmer foundation in Mormon theology and practice.

Above left: President Spencer W. Kimball greets visitors t[o]
Visitors' Center at the Mormon Temple in Washington, D.C., [a]
center's dedication in 1976. Part of the entourage, center, is a [former]
Administration cabinet member, David Kennedy, also a prom[inent]
Mormon. (Photo by Nelson Wadsworth)

Above right: New LDS Church President Harold B. Lee, cen[ter,]
congratulated after a solemn assembly sustained him in Salt [Lake]
City in 1972. Although he served only a few years, Presiden[t Lee]
was instrumental in streamlining management of the LDS enter[prise]
around the world and began construction of the Church's hig[h-rise]
office building and worldwide headquarters in Salt Lake City[, but]
he did not live to see the project completed. Also in the phot[o]
are Nathan Eldon Tanner, left, a first counselor from Canada; [Apos-]
tle Marion G. Romney, center left; and Spencer W. Kimball, [right,]
then President of the Council of the Twelve. (Photo by [Nelson]
Wadsworth)

Left: LDS President Spencer W. Kimball speaks at a bicent[ennial]
celebration in Washington, D.C., in 1976. President Kimball[,]
known around the world for his humanitarian efforts for L[amanites]
and other impoverished people, served for more than a decade [until]
his death in 1985. (Photo by Nelson Wadsworth)

Opposite right: Mormons meeting in solemn assembly in th[e Salt]
Lake Tabernacle in 1972 raise their right arms to the square to [sustain]
Harold B. Lee as President of the LDS Church. (Photo by [Nelson]
Wadsworth)

Overleaf, page 283: Ezra Taft Benson, then President of the C[ouncil]
of Twelve Apostles, greets a Mormon family at a confere[nce in]
Stockholm, Sweden, in 1974. (Photo by J.M. Heslop, The [Deseret]
News)

*E*PILOGUE

*B*ut what of the future? There seems little reason to dispute Rodney Stark's assumption that the Mormon church will grow and take a place among the prominent world religions. Still, it will not happen without challenges and opposition. Throughout its history, Mormonism has had a full measure of groups and "sects" that have broken off from the main body. Some objected to Joseph Smith's leadership and doctrines; some found Brigham Young's economic ideas too unyielding while many wished to continue polygamy. None seems to have done significant permanent damage to the church and several crusades against Mormonism, past and present, have been a positive good. Mormons have been able to deal with persecution; it remains to be seen whether they can handle prosperity.

The prospects are, however, encouraging. Mormons throughout the world today are still bound together by their faithful adherence to the basic doctrines revealed to Joseph Smith. Together with the continued doctrines of divine priesthood authority and continuous revelation they form a basic canon of faith that all Mormons share. In addition, the millenarian tradition lives on; they share a pride in their history and a conviction of a future when Christ will come again to rule in power and glory.

Mormons, however, face many of the same problems of others around the world. They must contend with drugs, divorce, selfishness in all its forms, sexual deviancy and perversions, fraud, worldliness, and challenges to faith in a secular society. In the latter part of the twentieth century, the life-style of Mormons has changed dramatically from that of their pioneer forefathers. Most Mormons now live in cities in the United States and around the world. A large and ever-growing percentage have received a good education and are able to compete in a world moving into the Information Revolution.

But becoming a world faith brings not only recognition, but also unique burdens with which Mormons must seriously deal. Besides continuing the achievements of the past century and a half, being a world faith means having a world conscience; a prophet is for all of mankind, not just for a few. He can lead Mormons to a broader view of their worldwide Christian responsibilities. The world they live in can be made safer and better by their expanded institutional and individual cooperation with men and women of good will working toward similar goals. They can contribute not only by bringing the "gospel of peace" into more lives and hearts, but also by using a growing moral capital, as in the MX case, to promote general peace in the world.

They can also provide leadership, support, and inspiration in combating world hunger, physical and moral epidemics, and in promoting world literacy and joining their voices in support of the basic human rights and freedoms they cherish and which many throughout the world do not have. Mormons might also open themselves more to the world by letting the world, through the media and the scholarly world, see more closely what they are and believe. These are some opportunities and perhaps duties of one-time sect now becoming a world faith.

Mormonism continues today to offer meaningful answers to the "perennial questions"; it combines continuity and change, timeless absolutes, and the latest communication technology side by side. Modern Mormons live in a vastly different world, but share the same faith as Joseph Smith, Brigham Young, and Jacob Tobler. Mormons still believe that God is not dead, that He is still in charge of the world, that Jesus Christ, his resurrected son, atoned for all of our sins, and that the Ten Commandments and Sermon on the Mount are timeless truths. They still believe that Joseph Smith was God's prophet through whom the restoration of Christ's original church was brought about. Mormons also believe that Joseph's successors have the same prophetic calling and mission, and that all people should pay attention to their message. Mormons continue to find their faith confirmed through personal revelation and spiritual experiences and believe that these, together with scriptural truth, provide the understanding and motivation to live a life of happiness here and salvation hereafter.

TIME LINE

1805: Joseph Smith, Jr., the son of Joseph Smith, Sr., and Lucy Mack, was born on December 23 in Sharon, Vermont.

1811: The Smith family moved to Palmyra, New York.

1820: Fourteen-year-old Joseph had the first of many visions.

1830: The Book of Mormon, which Joseph had translated from ancient records, was published on March 26. On April 6 the Church of Jesus Christ of Latter-day Saints was officially founded.

1831: The first Mormons moved from upstate New York to Kirtland, Ohio, and Jackson County, Missouri.

1836: The first temple was dedicated in Kirtland on March 27.

1837: Mormonism was introduced to Britain and Europe.

1838: Joseph Smith and other church leaders were jailed in Liberty, Missouri.

1838/39: Mormons moved from Missouri to Illinois under the leadership of Brigham Young. The city of Nauvoo was founded.

1840: Mormon converts in Europe begin to emigrate to America.

1841: Cornerstone laying of Nauvoo Temple.

1844: Joseph Smith and his brother, Hyrum, were murdered by a mob on June 27 in Carthage, Illinois.

1846: Mormons leave Nauvoo and begin the trek west. They arrive in Salt Lake Valley in July, 1847.

1852: The doctrine of polygamy is taught publicly for the first time.

1869: The transcontinental railroad is completed on April 10 with the driving of the "golden spike" at Promontory, Utah.

1875: Brigham Young University was founded.

1882: The Edmunds-Tucker Act, which disfranchised the Church and sent polygamous Mormon men to prison, was passed by Congress.

1890: President Wilford Woodruff announced the end of polygamy with the Woodruff Manifesto in October.

1893: The temple in Salt Lake City was completed and dedicated.

1896: Utah was admitted as a state to the Union.

1936: The Church Welfare Program was introduced to aid the unemployed and needy in the Church during the Depression. This program later sent Care Packages to Europe after World War II.

1951: David O. McKay became President of the Church.

1955: The first temple outside of North America was dedicated in Bern, Switzerland.

1973: Church membership had grown to more than 3 million.

1978: President Spencer W. Kimball announced that the Priesthood would be given to blacks.

1985: The first Temple was built in a communist country in Freiberg, German Democratic Republic.

1986: Church membership passed the 6 million mark.

The Mormon Temple in Friedrichsdorf, near Frankfurt, West Germany, is pictured at the time of its dedication in 1987. The Frankfurt Temple is one of the Church's newest.

Notes

1. For detailed accounts of some of these pioneer photographers in the West, see Weston J. Naef and James N. Wood, *Era of Exploration* (Boston: New York Graphic Society, 1975); Nelson B. Wadsworth, *Through Camera Eyes* (Provo, Utah: Brigham Young University Press, 1975); Don D. Fowler, ed., *Photographed All the Best Scenery: Jack Hillers's Diary of the Powell Expeditions, 1871–1875* (Salt Lake City: University of Utah Press, 1972); James D. Horan, *Timothy O'Sullivan, America's Forgotten Photographer* (New York: Bonanza Books, 1966); Clarence S. Jackson, *Picture Maker of the Old West* (New York, 1947).

2. Clifton C. Edom, *Photojournalism Principles and Practices*, 2nd ed. (Dubuque, Iowa: Wm. C. Brown Co., 1980), p. 10.

3. Brigham H. Roberts, *A Comprehensive History of The Church of Jesus Christ of Latter-day Saints, Century I*, 6 vols. (Provo, Utah: Brigham Young University Press), 1:394.

4. Beaumont Newhall, *The Daguerreotype in America* (Greenwich, Conn.: New York Graphic Society, 1961). For Daguerre's description of the process, see page 19.

5. For a description of an excellent copying technique, see Newhall, page 134. Because the mirror-like images are inherently flat, we discovered it is best to enhance the contrast as much as possible through the time and temperature method of development. To do this, underexpose the copy film slightly and overdevelop to increase the contrast. We used Kodak Ektapan (ASA 100) in a 4 by 5 Graphic view camera with a F/7.7 Ektar lens and followed Newhall's suggestions on unpolarized lighting and copy board techniques. We also discovered the contrast can be further improved by making duplicate negatives on Kodak SO-15 Direct Positive Duplicating Film, following the manufacturer's recommendations. The duplicated negatives, we found, produced better prints than the Ektapan master.

6. For a philosophical discussion on the visual image of Joseph Smith, see Wadsworth, pages 7–12, and William B. McCarl, "The Visual Image of Joseph Smith" (Master's thesis, Brigham Young University, 1962).

7. Eugene Ostroff, *Conserving and Restoring Photographic Collections* (Washington, D.C.: American Association of Museums, 1976), p. 12. The technique for "Cleaning Daguerreotypes" described is the one most accepted by conservators, but even Ostroff admits the risks involved.

8. Irving Pobboravsky, "Daguerreotype Preservation: The Problems of Tarnish Removal," *Technology and Conservation*, Summer 1978. Pobboravsky's conclusion was that daguerreotype images are permanently altered by any known cleaning process and more research must be done before they can be cleaned with a minimum of risk.

9. James M. Reilly, *The Albumen & Salted Paper Book, The History and Practice of Photographic Printing, 1840–1895* (Rochester, N.Y.: Light Impressions, 1980), preface.

10. Robert Taft, *Photography and the American Scene* (New York: Dover Publications, 1938), p. 248.

11. Wadsworth, p. 16.

12. Henry Wilhelm, "Color Print Instability," *Modern Photography*, February 1979, p. 93.

13. Frederick Hawkins Piercy, *Route from Liverpool to Great Salt Lake Valley*, ed. Fawn Brodie (reprint ed., Cambridge, Mass.: Harvard University Press, 1962).

14. Author's interview with Anderson's oldest daughter, Eva Noyes, fall of 1974, in her home in Salt Lake City.

15. For a commentary on Anderson's life, including details of his work on Church sites, see Wadsworth, pages 159–170.

16. John Henry Evans, *The Birth of Mormonism in Picture* (Denver, Colo.: Williamson-Haffner Co., 1909).

17. Two earlier prominent German scholars, Moritz Busch in 1869 and Eduard Meyer in 1912,

had also been fascinated by the Mormons and their doctrines. They are typical of the nineteenth century European intellectual view of Mormons and Mormonism. Busch had marveled at the dedication of the missionaries, the growth of the church in the face of persecution, and the later founding of the Mormon kingdom in the West. Mormon teachings including the corporeality of God and the idea that man can become a god, constituted ". . . wohl das seltsamste Credo, welches seit Jahrhunderten im Bereiche der christichen Welt aufgetaucht ist." (Busch, V) But Busch considered the Mormon Kingdom also "Asiatic" because of polygamy and predicted that with the coming of more educated non-Mormons, Utah would return to being American.

For Meyer, Mormonism was a new *Offenbarungsreligion*, (religion based on revelation) similar to Islam, whose study was warranted because it was "one of the crudest and intellectually most primitive" in the world, "eine der rohesten, ja vielleicht die intellectuell am tiefsten stehend." (Meyer, 1)

18.   That all polygamous families were not quite this harmonious can be seen from the journal of C. Anderson who later served with a large group of Mormon men seventeen months in prison for his loyalty to the "principle" of polygamy.

On November 30, 1876, he recorded his lamentations on the death of his wife, Anna Kirstine:

Before she died she called for my wife Rasmine; she wanted to see her before she died, but when Rasmine came she could not tell her anything, the power of speech had left her. Rasmine hated her and had acted very jealous and made us a great deal of trouble by her jealousy and ungovernable temper and malice.

My wife, Anna Kirstine, was in her 21st year when she died; she was below medium height, well-proportioned, was of a mental-vital temperament, of fair complexion, was very playful, cheerful, loving, easily governed, exceedingly orderly and cleanly [*sic*] as well as industrious and economical. I felt that her death was the greatest calamity that had ever befallen me. I had no peaceable home now to go to. All my comfort and consolation I must seek outside my home. (Anderson, private journal)

ℬIBLIOGRAPHY

Alder, Douglas D. "The German-Speaking Immigration to Utah." Master's thesis, University of Utah, Salt Lake City, Utah, 1958.

Alexander, Thomas G., and James B. Allen. *Mormons and Gentiles: A History of Salt Lake City*. Boulder, Colo.: Pruett Publishing Co., 1984.

Allen, James B. "With a Strong Hand: The Life and Leadership of David O. McKay." Manuscript.

Allen, James B., and Glen M. Leonard. *The Story of the Latter-day Saints*. Salt Lake City: Deseret Book, 1976.

Anderson, Christian. Private journal.

Arrington, Leonard J. *Brigham Young: American Moses*. New York: Alfred A. Knopf, 1985.

Arrington, Leonard J., and Davis Bitton. *The Mormon Experience*. New York: Vintage, 1980.

Baumer, Franklin. *Modern European Thought: Continuity and Change in Ideas, 1600–1950*. New York: Macmillan, 1977.

Benz, Ernst. "Der Mensch als Imago Dei." In *Urbild und Abbild: Der Mensch und die mythische Welt*. Leiden: E.J. Brill, 1974.

Busch, Moritz. *Geschichte der Mormonen nebst einen Darslellung ihres Glaubens und ihrer gegen wärtigen socialen und politischen Verhältnisse*. Leipzig: Verlag von Ambrosius Abel, 1869.

Bushman, Richard L. *Joseph Smith and the Beginnings of Mormonism*. Urbana and Chicago: University of Illinois Press, 1984.

Clark, James R. *Messages of the First Presidency of the Church of Jesus Christ of Latter-day Saints*. Salt Lake City: Bookcraft, 1975.

Cowley, Matthias F. *Wilford Woodruff, Fourth President of the Church . . . History of His Life and Labors as Recorded in His Daily Journals*. Salt Lake City: Deseret News, 1909.

Cracroft, Richard H. "Ten Wives Is All You Need: Artemus Twain and The Mormons—Again." *Western Humanities Review* 38 (Autumn 1984):197–211.

Doctrine and Covenants of the Church of Jesus Christ of Latter-day Saints. Containing Revelations Given to Joseph Smith the Prophet With Some Additions By His Successors in the Presidency of the Church. Salt Lake City: Church of Jesus Christ of Latter-day Saints, 1981.

Godfrey, Kenneth W., Audrey M. Godfrey, and Jill Mulvay Derr. *Women's Voices: An Untold History of the Latter-day Saints, 1830–1900*. Salt Lake City: Deseret Book, 1982.

Hafen, Leroy, and Ann W. Hafen. *Handcarts to Zion: The Story of a Unique Western Migration, 1856–1860*. Glendale, California: Arthur H. Clark, 1960.

Hinckley, Bryant S. "Greatness in Men: President Heber J. Grant." *Improvement Era* 34–42 (October 1931):701–703, 733.

"History of Brigham Young." *Millenial Star*, November 26, 1864.

Jensen, Andrew. *Latter-day Saint Biographical Encyclopedia*. Salt Lake City: Andrew Jensen History Co., 1901. Reprint, Western Epics, 1971.

Jones, Dan. *History of the Latter-day Saints, From Their Establishment in 1823 Until the Time That 300,000 of Them Were Exiled From America Because of Their Religion in 1846*. Translation of Welsh Title by Ronald D. Dennis. Merthyr Tydfil: Published and for sale by Capt. Jones, 1847.

Journal of Discourses. Liverpool, 1854–1886. 26 vols.

Kimball, Stanley B. *Heber C. Kimball: Mormon Patriarch and Pioneer*. Urbana: University of Illinois Press, 1981.

Koontz, David. "The Mormon Welfare Relief to Europe, 1946–1949." Manuscript in preparation.

"LDS Church Leaders Oppose MX." *Deseret News*, May 7, 1981.

LDS Conference Reports, Annual, April 1925–1928.

Lively, Robert L. Jr. "The Catholic Apostolic Church and the Church of Jesus Christ of Latter-day Saints: A Comparative Study of Two Minority Millenarian Groups in Nineteenth Century England." Ph.D. dissertation, Oxford, 1977.

Maeser, Reinhard. *Karl G. Maeser: A Biography.* Provo, Utah: Brigham Young University, 1928.

Maxwell, Neal A. "Spencer, The Beloved: Leader-Servant." *Ensign* 15 (December 1985):8–19.

Meyer, Edward. *Ursprung und Geschichte der Mormonen.* Haale A. Soale: Verlag von Max Niemeyer, 1912.

Mulder, William, and A. Russell Mortensen (eds.) *Among the Mormons: Historic Accounts by Contemporary Observers.* Lincoln: University of Nebraska Press, 1973.

Poll, Richard D., Thomas G. Alexander, et al. *Utah's History.* Provo, Utah: Brigham Young University Press, 1978.

Scharffs, Gilbert W. *Mormonism in Germany: A History of the Church of Jesus Christ of Latter-day Saints in Germany Between 1840 and 1970.* Salt Lake City: Deseret Book, 1970.

Shipps, Jan. *Mormonism: The Story of a New Religious Tradition.* Urbana and Chicago: University of Illinois Press, 1985.

Smith, Joseph. *History of the Church of Jesus Christ of Latter-day Saints.* Introduction and notes by B.H. Roberts. 2nd rev. ed. Salt Lake City: Deseret Book, 1976.

Smith, Joseph F. "Congress and the Mormons." *Improvement Era* 6 (June 1903):469–473.

Smith, Joseph Fielding. *Teachings of the Prophet Joseph Smith.* Salt Lake City: Deseret Book, 1972.

Sonne, Conway B. *Saints of the Seas: A Maritime History of Mormon Migration, 1830–1890.* Salt Lake City: University of Utah Press, 1983.

Spencer, Orson. *Letters Exhibiting the Most Prominent Doctrines of the Church of Jesus Christ of Latter-day Saints.* Liverpool: 1848.

Stark, Rodney. "The Rise of a New World Faith." *Review of Religious Research* 26 (September 1984):18–27.

Stegner, Wallace. *The Gathering to Zion.* New York: McGraw-Hill, 1964.

Talmage, James E. Unpublished journal (Brigham Young University Library).

Tobler, Douglas F. "Karl G. Maeser's German Background, 1828–1856: The Making of Zion's Teacher." *Zeitschrift für Religious—und Geistesgeschichte* Bd. XXIX, Heft 4 (1977), 325–344.

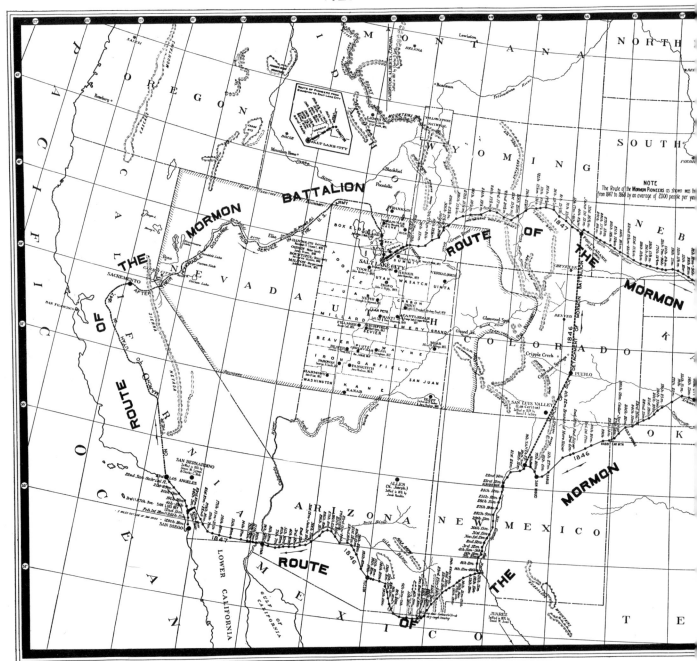